ECONOMIC AND SOCIAL COMMISSION FOR ASIA AND THE PACIFIC

STATISTICAL PROFILES   No. 17

WOMEN IN JAPAN

A COUNTRY PROFILE

UNITED NATIONS
New York, 1998

ST/ESCAP/1770

UNITED NATIONS PUBLICATION
Sales No. E.99.II.F.25
Copyright © United Nations 1999
ISBN: 92-1-119892-5

The views expressed in this profile are those of the author and do not necessarily reflect those of the United Nations. The designations employed and the presentation of the material in this publication do not imply the expression of any opinion whatsoever on the part of the Secretariat of the United Nations concerning the legal status of any country, territory, city or area, or of its authorities, or concerning the delimitation of its frontiers or boundaries. Mention of firm names and commercial products does not imply the endorsement of the United Nations.

In the tables, two dots (..) indicate that data are not available, a dash (–) indicates nil or negligible, and a blank that the item is not applicable.

The profile has been prepared under project BK-X20-3-214, on improving statistics on women in the ESCAP region.

FOREWORD

The call for the development of statistics and indicators on the situation of women has, for some time, been voiced in various global and regional forums. It was first recommended by the World Plan of Action for the Implementation of the Objectives of the International Women's Year, adopted in 1975. The recommendations of the World Plan of Action were reaffirmed and elaborated in the Programme of Action for the Second Half of the United Nations Decade for Women: Equality, Development and Peace. On various occasions, the Commission, stressing the importance of social and human development, has recognized the need for improved statistics and indicators on women. It has noted that better indicators are required to monitor the situation of women and to assess the effectiveness of strategies and programmes designed to address priority gender issues.

The secretariat initiated the project on improving statistics on women in the ESCAP region in 1994. The project aims to support governments in their efforts to promote the full integration of women in development and improve their status in line with the Nairobi Forward-looking Strategies for the Advancement of Women adopted in 1985. The project has been implemented by the Economic and Social Commission for Asia and the Pacific (ESCAP) through its subprogramme on statistics, with funding assistance from the Government of the Netherlands.

As a major component of its activities, the project commissioned experts from 19 countries in the region to prepare country profiles on the situation of women and men in the family, at work, and in public life, by analysing available statistical data and information. The profiles are intended to highlight the areas where action is needed, and to raise the consciousness of readers about issues concerning women and men. The 19 countries are Bangladesh, China, India, Indonesia, the Islamic Republic of Iran, Japan, Nepal, Pakistan, the Philippines, the Republic of Korea, Sri Lanka and Thailand in Asia; and Cook Islands, Fiji, Papua New Guinea, Samoa, Solomon Islands, Tonga and Vanuatu in the Pacific.

The secretariat hosted two meetings each in Asia and in the Pacific as part of the project activities. In the first meeting, the experts discussed and agreed on the structure, format and con-tents of the country profiles, based on guidelines prepared by the secretariat through Ms C.N. Ericta, consultant. The second meeting was a workshop to review the draft profiles. Participants in the workshop included the country experts and invited representatives from national statistical offices of Brunei Darussalam; Hong Kong, China; the Lao People's Democratic Republic; Mongolia; and Viet Nam in Asia; of Marshall Islands; Tuvalu; and Vanuatu in the Pacific; and representatives of United Nations organizations, specialized agencies and international organizations.

The original draft of the present profile, *Women in Japan,* was prepared by Ms Machiko Osawa, Professor of Economics, Asia University. It was technically edited and modified by the ESCAP secretariat with the assistance of Mr S. Selvaratnam, consultant. The profiles express the views of the author and not necessarily those of the secretariat.

I wish to express my sincere appreciation to the Government of the Netherlands for its generous financial support, which enabled the secretariat to implement the project.

Adrianus Mooy
Executive Secretary

CONTENTS

LIST OF TABLES

LIST OF FIGURES

LIST OF ANNEX TABLES

PART I
DESCRIPTIVE ANALYSIS

INTRODUCTION

In traditional Japanese society, with its mixture of Buddhist and Confucian ideals and influences, women were regarded as inferior to men in ability and competence. The role of women within the family was merely that of a home-maker: to raise children; to assume responsibility for domestic chores; and to serve their husbands with complete submission. Under the then multi-generational household system, women's rights were artificially restricted; they could not legally own or control property, or even select their spouses.

However, the situation has changed dramatically over the years owing to rapid modernization, migration and urbanization, as well as the increasing opportunities for women's education and employment outside the home. The thinking and attitudes of Japanese people have also been moving gradually towards gender equality. Successive national governments have been adopting a series of legal and policy measures and establishing relevant institutional and administrative arrangements to facilitate the enhancement of women's status in the family and society.

The 1946 Constitution guarantees basic human rights such as respect for individuals and equality between women and men. Under the Nationality Law enacted in 1950, women have the same rights as men in regard to the acquisition and termination of Japanese nationality. The 1980 Amendments to the Civil Code improved the status of women in regard to inheritance substantially by increasing the spouse's legal share of the estate and by establishing procedures for the division of the estate according to the inheritor's contribution to the property of the deceased. Consequent upon the enactment of the Equal Employment Opportunity Act in 1985, women now enjoy legislative guarantees of equality in regard to recruitment, assignment, promotion, vocational training, and fringe and retirement benefits.

The Government of Japan is also a signatory to several international covenants relating to women. In 1967, Japan ratified ILO Convention No. 100 on Equal Remuneration for Men and Women Workers for Work of Equal Value, and the principle of equal pay for equal work regardless of the sex of the worker has been incorporated in the country's Labour Standards Law. Japan ratified the United Nations Convention on the Elimination of All Forms of Discrimination Against Women in June 1985.

A high-level coordinating mechanism emerged in 1975 when the Government established the Headquarters for the Planning and Promoting of Policies Relating to Women. This body, which is presided over by the Prime Minister, includes the vice-ministers of agencies and ministries concerned with women's affairs, namely, the Prime Minister's Office, the Economic Planning Agency, and the ministries of agriculture, education, finance, foreign affairs, health and welfare, home affairs, justice, and labour. The Office of Women's Affairs under the Prime Minister's Office serves as the secretariat of the Headquarters. In addition, there is an Advisory Council to the Prime Minister on Women's Affairs. At the local level, the governments of the 47 prefectures and 10 designated cities have special sections responsible for women's concerns.

Non-governmental organizations (NGOs) have also responded to the calls of international agencies by working actively to enhance the status of Japanese women. These NGOs include general organizations, professional associations, and the women's wings of labour unions and political parties. In the course of the International Women's Year, NGOs formed a liaison group consisting of major women's organizations. Since 1975, this group has organized five-yearly national conventions at which progress has been assessed and decisions made on further activities that need to be undertaken in accord with the major projects of the United Nations.

In 1977, the Government, in collaboration with the NGOs, issued a National Plan of Action which outlined comprehensive measures to be undertaken during the next 10 years in order to advance the status of Japanese women in all areas. Special importance was attached in the Plan to the improvement of the legal status of women; acceleration of women's participation in every field on an equal footing with men; respect for motherhood and protection of maternal health; greater security for older persons and the promotion of international cooperation. In a programme prepared in 1981, the Government identified nine priority areas for the second half of the decade.

In 1987, the New National Plan of Action Towards the Year 2000 was formulated. Based on the recommendations and conclusions arising from the first review and appraisal of the Nairobi Forward-looking Strategies for the Advancement of Women the First Revision of the New National Plan of Action was effected in 1991. In accordance with these revisions, the Plan outlined basic policies for the period 1987-2000 and concrete measures for the period 1991-1995, and recommended the formulation of further concrete measures from 1996 onwards.

In 1994, the year prior to the Fourth World Conference on Women, held in Beijing, Japan reorganized its Headquarters for the Planning and Promoting of Policies Relating to Women, and renamed it the Headquarters for the Promotion of Gender Equality. The new Headquarters, presided over by the Prime Minister, includes the Chief Cabinet Secretary and Minister for Women's Affairs as Vice-President, and all cabinet ministers as members. In addition, the Council for Gender Equality was established as an advisory body to the Prime Minister.

In August 1994, the Prime Minister requested the Council for Gender Equality to formulate an "Overall Vision of a Gender-equal Society Towards the Twenty-first Century". In July 1996, based on studies and deliberations that incorporated a broad cross-section of public opinion and the recommendations of the Fourth World Conference on Women, the Council presented its conclusions in a report entitled "Vision of gender equality". This report spelled out the definition, ideals and aims of a gender-equal society and proposed a direction and an agenda to be pursued until the year 2010 based on economic and social changes in Japan.

The report also pinpointed five areas requiring action to ensure the achievement of a gender-equal society: systems and customs that lead to gender-related prejudices; existing inequalities between women and men in the family, community and workplace; gross under-representation of women in the policy and decision-making processes; inadequate efforts to promote/defend the right to live without discrimination on the basis of gender; and the need for increasing positive action toward the realization of "equality, development and peace" in the global community.

The "Vision of gender equality" also proposed specific measures to address the challenges and constraints mentioned above, and emphasized the need to establish and strengthen structures for the comprehensive and effective promotion of these measures. As an integral part of these efforts, the report also emphasized the need for the regular and systematic collection of statistical data and information to evaluate and analyse the impact of various policies and programmes, and to make available such data and information to national and local-level governments, NGOs and others through various information networks.

Fortunately, Japan continues to collect and analyse a mass of data and information relevant to women's issues. The present profile on women in Japan has been prepared on the basis of data and information available through various sources.

A. HIGHLIGHTS

The setting

1. Because of the largely mountainous and rugged terrain in Japan, only about 30 per cent of its land area of 377,829 km^2 is habitable. The extreme scarcity of level land is one of the important features of the geography of the country.

2. Japan has a parliamentary system of government with the Cabinet of Ministers, headed by the Prime Minister, being responsible for the day-to-day management of the country's affairs. All judicial power is vested with the Supreme Court headed by a Chief Justice.

3. For convenience of administration, the country is divided into 47 prefectures and 3,233 municipalities. The 12 largest cities are designated as cities having administrative and fiscal powers similar to those of prefectural governments.

4. According to the latest census held in 1995, the population of Japan was 125.6 million and growing at an annual rate of 0.3 per cent. This rate, one of the lowest in the world, has been brought about by a sharper decline in fertility compared with mortality. Nearly 77 per cent of the population reside in urban areas.

5. Japanese people are ethnically and linguistically homogeneous, except for the small minority groups. The traditional religions of the people are Buddhism and Shintoism.

6. Japan is a highly developed country and a major industrial power in the world. Industry (including manufacture, construction, mining and utilities) continues to be the dominant economic sector.

7. The national education and the country's health services are well developed, but housing is still inadequate compared with Western industrialized countries.

Women's profile

1. Since the 1940s, females have consistently outnumbered males in total population, but there is a slight excess of males over females at younger ages.

2. Drastic reductions in fertility and mortality over the years have resulted in the transition from a "young" to an "ageing" population. The relative share of older persons in the total population increased unprecedentedly between 1950 and 1995, and the ageing process is more pronounced among females than among males.

3. The proportion remaining single or unmarried among males and females aged 15 years and over has been increasing in recent years. The percentage of the population living in a state of marital disruption – widowed or divorced – is considerably higher among females than among males.

4. The participation of women in the education system has increased over the years, resulting in enrolment ratios for girls being either equal to or higher than that of boys in elementary and secondary schools. But women continue to be significantly under-represented in various tertiary educational institutions, excepting the junior colleges.

5. As in most other countries of the region, there is a tendency for sex-stereotyping in regard to the selection of study areas. Generally, women are concentrated in arts-based courses, while the preference of male students is for science-based studies.

6. Women have also been participating increasingly in the education process as teachers, and today they constitute the majority of elementary school teachers and more than a third of the teaching staff in lower secondary schools and junior colleges. But women are grossly under-represented in the faculties of technical colleges and universities.

7. The level of educational attainment of the adult population aged 25 years and over has been increasing over the years. However, the proportion with secondary or post-secondary education is higher among men than among women.

8. Over the years, there has been a drastic reduction in the incidence of diseases and deaths, but this decline has been accompanied by a shift in the pattern of morbidity from one dominated by infectious and contagious diseases to one in which non-communicable lifestyle diseases constitute the major causes of morbidity and mortality.

9. Infant and mortality rates have declined dramatically and the current levels rank among

the lowest in the world. Female death rates are lower than male rates at all ages.

10. Average life expectancy at birth has been rising over the years and today Japan has the highest average longevity in the world. Japanese females have a significatly higher life expectancy compared with Japanese males.

Women in family life

1. Rapid modernization and urbanization have led to radical transformation in the Japanese household/family system. The traditional extended family/household is being increasingly replaced by nuclear and single-member family households. Consequently, average family size has been declining over the years.

2. There have also been very significant changes in marriage practices and patterns. Marriages based on romantic love have re-emerged in a big way, together with an increasing tendency among young persons to delay their marriage. Consequently, the proportions remaining unmarried at younger ages as well as the mean age at first marriage have been rising over the years among both males and females.

3. Since the early part of this century, the attitudes of married couples regarding desired family size have undergone significant shifts, as evidenced by the dramatic decline in the number of children parents produce. The total fertility rate declined from 5.24 in 1920 to 4.6 in 1993.

4. The contraceptive prevalence rate has increased markedly since 1950. Japan has the highest rate of condom use among the world's industrialized countries, accounting for about 80 per cent of all modern methods in use.

5. Despite the increase in the contraceptive prevalence rate, a significant proportion of married couples continue to resort to induced aboution to terminate unwanted pregnancies.

6. Marital disruption due to divorce has been increasing in recent years, the proportions

divorced being significantly higher for females than for males at all ages.

7. The number of fatherless families has also been increasing in recent years. Divorce, not the demise of the father, has emerged as the leading cause of fatherless households.

Women in economic life

1. Although women constitute more than 50 per cent of the persons in the working ages, they are considerably under-represented in the country's workforce. In 1995, the female labour-force participation rate of 50.0 per cent was 27.6 percentage points lower than the male rate.

2. The vast majority of employed males and females are engaged in the tertiary industrial sectors, and the most important sources of employment for female workers are the service and trade sectors.

3. Nearly 30 per cent of employed females are clerical and related workers, and another 20 per cent are craftsmen, mining, production process and construction workers, and labourers.

4. A higher proportion among employed females (76.1 per cent) compared with employed males (74.8 per cent) are engaged as paid employees. But a third of the female paid employees are part-time workers, and the growth of female part-time employment has outpaced that of overall female employment in recent years.

5. The wages and remuneration received by female workers are, on the average, considerably lower than those paid to their male counterparts in all sectors of the economy and in all forms of employment.

6. In recent years, the unemployment rates have been rising owing to the recession experienced by the Japanese economy, and there are indications of blatant discrimination against women in regard to recruitment.

Women in public life

1.   In Japan, women have consistently out-numbered men as registered or eligible voters as well as actual voters at the various national and local-level elections.   Nevertheless, they are very much under-represented in the various representative or legislative bodies.

2.   Since women constitute only about 7 per cent of the total membership of the parliament (Diet), they are also grossly under-represented in the Cabinet and in the various standing committees.

3.   Although measures have been adopted to increase the number of women employees in government ministries and agencies, women constituted only about 15 per cent of all regular public service employees in 1992.   Nearly 58 per cent of the female government employees are in the lowest levels of the service, the corresponding proportion among males being 35 per cent.

4.   Women are also very much under-represented in the Special Defence Force (SDF) and the police, with only 3.8 per cent of all SDF personnel and 2.5 per cent of all police officers being female in the early 1990s.

5.   The judicial system in Japan is male-dominated; only abut 6 per cent of the practising lawyers, 3 per cent of the public prosecutors, and 7 per cent of the judges are women.

6.   Despite various measures taken to promote women's participation in the decision-making process, women constitute only about 12 per cent of the membership of national advisory councils and committees.

B.   THE SETTING

1.   Location and physical features

Japan forms a curved chain of islands off the north-eastern coast of the Asian continent stretching from latitude 45°N to latitude 30°N. It consists of four large islands, named (from north to south) Hokkaido, Honshu, Shikoku and Kyusyu, which together constitute 98 per cent of the national territory; over 3,000 small adjacent islands and islets; and the Ryukyui Islands, including Okinawa and many other smaller islands.   The four major islands extend to a distance of approximately 1,400 miles and the Ryukyu Islands stretch another 600 miles in a generally south-westerly direction from Kyusyu.

The total area of the country is 145,877 square miles, or 377,829 km^2.   Much of the terrain is mountainous and rugged; forests cover about 69 per cent of the country.   Lowland plain areas, which are generally fertile and productive, are relatively few and separated by mountain regions.   The extreme scarcity of level land is one of the important features of the geography of Japan.

Japan is characterized by complex topographical features, including a prominent "spine" of mountains in Honshu, where Mt. Fuji (3,776 meters high) is the highest and most famous peak.   There are three major zones of active volcanoes and hot springs in Hokkaido, in northern and central Honshu, and in southern Kyusyu.   The islands experience over 1,000 tremors every year.

2.   Climate and rainfall

Since Japan stretches over 15 degrees of latitude, the four main islands have regional climatic variations that range from subtropical in Kyusyu to cool temperate in Hokkaido. Japanese summers are sufficiently warm and humid to permit the widespread cultivation of paddy, yet cold, dry winters clearly differentiate Japan from those countries of subtropical and tropical Asia, where constant and high temperatures inhibit prolonged human effort.   In August, temperatures average about 70°F in the northernmost part of the island of Hokkaido and 77°F in Honshu.   Central and south-western Japan have a humid subtropical climate, the temperatures during the warmest months averaging between 75°F and 81°F (see figure 1).

Rainfall is generally adequate throughout Japan; annual precipitation varies from 33 inches in eastern Hokkaido to over 120 inches in the mountains of central Honshu and in those parts of the Pacific coast which are fully exposed to the force of the late summer typhoons which usually hit Japan several times from July to October (see figure 1).

Figure 1. Temperature and precipitation (1961-1990 average)

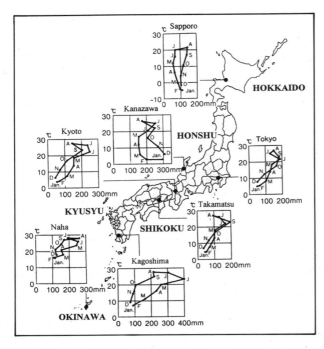

Source: Statistics Bureau, *Statistical Handbook of Japan, 1996.*

3. Government and administration

Under the provisions of the Constitution, which has been in force since May 1947, the Emperor is the Head of State but has no governing power. Legislative power is vested with the bicameral Diet (parliament) comprising the House of Representatives, or lower house, and the House of Councillors, or upper house. All 500 members of the lower house and the 252 members of the upper house are elected under a system of universal suffrage for all Japanese adults aged 20 years and over. The members of the House of Representatives are elected for a four-year term, while the Councillors are elected for six years, half of them being elected every three years.

The House of Representatives enjoys more authority than the House of Councillors in regard to the selection of the Prime Minister, in passing the national budget and in approving international treaties. Legislation is drafted by government bureaucrats before being steered through the two chambers by the administration in a process that often involves the use of joint committees to resolve disagreements.

The executive power is vested with the Cabinet headed by the Prime Minster, who is formally appointed by the Emperor upon designation by the Diet. The Prime Minister himself appoints 20 Ministers of State who form the Cabinet. The Cabinet is collectively responsible to the Diet.

The Constitution vests all judicial power with the Supreme Court, the highest legal authority in the country, consisting of the Chief Justice and 14 associate justices. The Supreme Court administers eight high courts, below which are 452 summary courts, 50 district courts and 50 family courts. Judges are to be independent in the exercise of their conscience, and may not be removed except by public impeachment. The justices of the Supreme Court are appointed by the Cabinet, the sole exception being the Chief Justice, who is appointed by the Emperor on the recommendation of the Cabinet. There is no jury system, and judicial precedents are generally considered to be binding.

Japan has two levels of local government: prefectures, and municipalities (cities, towns and villages). As of 1 April 1996, there were 47 prefectures and 3,233 municipalities. Each prefecture is administered by a governor and a unicameral assembly, both elected by popular vote. The 12 largest cities are designated as cities having administrative and fiscal powers similar to those of prefectural governments. The powers and responsibilities of the local government institutions are outlined in the Local Autonomy Law which came into effect in 1947.

4. Population growth and distribution

The population of Japan, according to the first complete census conducted in 1920, was about 56 million. Since then it has been growing to reach about 125.6 million persons at the latest census held in 1995. In other words, the population more than doubled in 75 years (table 1). In terms of population size, Japan today ranks eighth in the world and fourth in the Asian region.

Table 1. Growth of the population: 1920-1995

Census year	Population (thousands)	Average annual rate of growth	Population density (per km^2)
1920	55 963	..	147
1925	59 737	1.3	156
1930	64 450	1.5	169
1935	69 254	1.4	181
1940	73 114	1.1	191
1945[a]	71 998	..	195
1950	84 115	..	226
1955	90 077	1.4	242
1960	94 302	0.9	253
1965	99 209	1.0	267
1970	104 665	1.1	281
1975	111 940	1.4	300
1980	117 060	0.9	314
1985	121 049	0.7	325
1990	123 611	0.4	332
1995	125 569	0.3	337

Source: Statistics Bureau, Management and Coordination Agency, Ministry of Health and Welfare.

[a] Excluding Okinawa Prefecture.

It will also be noted from table 1 that the population did not grow at a uniform rate throughout the 75 years from 1920 to 1995. The average annual growth rate fluctuated during the various intercensal periods, averaging about 1.4 per cent between 1920 and 1935, about 1.0 per cent between 1960 and 1970, rising to 1.4 per cent during the period 1970-1975, and thereafter declining gradually to reach a very low rate of 0.3 per cent a year during the intercensal period 1990-1995. The dramatic decline in population growth rate was due to a faster decline in fertility compared with mortality.

The birth rate in Japan reached a comparatively high level of around 19 per thousand population during the so-called "second baby boom" from 1971 to 1973, but since then it has declined sharply, registering its lowest level of 9.6 in 1993. The crude birth rate of 10.0 per thousand population in 1994 reflects the first increase in this rate in 21 years. In the same year, the total fertility rate, or the average number of children born to each woman, was 1.50. The crude death rate remained at a stable level of between 6.0 and 6.3 per thousand population from 1975 to 1987, but with the ageing of the population it began to rise again in 1988, reaching 7.1 in 1993 and 1994 (see also figure 2).

Figure 2. Trend in the birth rate, death rate and natural increase rate: 1947 to 1994

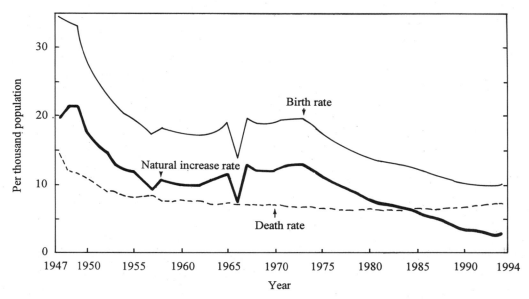

Source: Ministry of Health and Welfare.

9

The increase in population has inevitably resulted in an increase in population density, from 147 persons per km^2 in 1920 to 337 in 1995 (table 1). The current population density is one of the highest for countries with a population of over 5 million. The national average density, however, conceals the wide variation in population distribution across the country. As noted earlier, Japan is a mountainous country and only about 21 per cent of Japan's land area is habitable. Since the vast majority of the population live on one fifth of the total area, the population density of over 1,500 persons per km^2 of habitable land is undoubtedly the highest in the world.

The process of industrialization and urbanization beginning in the middle of the Meiji era has resulted in an uneven distribution of the population on the plains of Japan. In 1920, only 18.0 per cent of the population was residing in urban areas and the remaining 82 per cent in rural areas. But since then the urban population has been increasing rapidly, owing largely to rural-to-urban migration. In 1990, more than three quarters of the Japanese people were living in urban areas (table 2).

Table 2. Urban and rural population: 1920 to 1990

Year	Population (thousands)		Percentage	
	Urban	Rural	Urban	Rural
1920	10 097	45 866	18.0	82.0
1925	12 897	46 840	21.6	78.4
1930	15 444	49 006	24.0	76.0
1935	22 666	46 588	32.7	67.3
1940	27 578	45 537	37.7	62.3
1945	20 022	51 976	27.8	72.2
1950	31 366	52 749	37.3	62.7
1955	50 532	39 544	56.1	43.9
1960	59 678	34 622	63.3	36.7
1965	67 356	31 853	67.9	32.1
1970	75 429	29 237	72.1	27.9
1975	84 967	26 972	75.9	24.1
1980	89 187	27 873	76.2	23.8
1985	92 889	28 160	76.7	23.3
1990	95 644	27 968	77.4	22.6

Source: Statistics Bureau, Management and Coordination Agency.

As a result of the enormous increases in the urban population, particularly since 1955, nearly 42 per cent of the population was concentrated in three major metropolitan areas, or areas within a radius of 50 km from the city centres of Tokyo, Osaka and Nagoya. Since then, the proportion of the population in the Tokyo area has increased somewhat, but there have been almost negligible changes in respect of the other two metropolitan areas. Consequently, these three areas together accounted for 43.6 per cent of the country's population in 1990, and their population density in that year was considerably higher than the national average: Tokyo (3,831 persons per km^2); Osaka (2,183 per km^2) and Nagoya (1,150 per km^2).

5. Ethnicity and religion

The origin of the Japanese people is still uncertain, but they are predominantly Mongoloid in physical type. There is, however, a small group of indigenous people, the Ainu, who are considered by some to have descended from the early Caucasoid peoples of northern Asia, and by others to have Australo-Oceanic relationships. Over the years, the number of Ainu people has fallen, largely on account of mixed marriages, and is at present estimated to be around 25,000, most of whom reside in Hokkaido.

There are two other ethnic minority groups: the inhabitants of the Ryukyu Islands, generally referred to as Okinawans; and the Koreans. The Okinawans, who are usually regarded as different from the Japanese both ethnically and culturally, exhibit a more obvious Chinese influence, and number over a million persons. The Koreans, who number less than a million, are the descendants of the people brought to Japan as forced labourers before and during the Second World War. They have maintained their cultural identity and many still feel a close affinity for their homeland.

Except for the very small minority groups, the Japanese are ethnically and linguistically a homogeneous group of people who have been united for over a thousand years. This ethnic and linguistic homogeneity and the absence of any divisions based on race or language have been a very important factor in the rapidity and ease with which Japan achieved its modernization.

The traditional religions of Japan are Shintoism and Buddhism; neither is exclusive, and many Japanese subscribe at least nominally to both. Since 1945, a number of new religions have evolved, based on a fusion of Shinto, Buddhist, Daoist, Confucian and Christian beliefs.

6. The economy

With an average per capita gross national product (GNP) estimated at $34,630 during the period 1992-1994, Japan continues to rank among the highly developed nations and major industrial powers in the world. In terms of total gross domestic product (GDP), its economy is the second largest in the world after the United States of America and, in terms of GDP and GDP per head, Japan is the first among the G.7 countries (see figure 3).

The Japanese economy experienced a period of sustained economic growth in the 1980s based on strong export performance. Although its GDP increased in real terms by an annual average of 3.5 per cent during the period 1980-1993, there was a marked deceleration during the period 1991-1993, with the industrial sector recording a 4.5 per cent decrease in production in 1993 and real GDP registering zero growth in the same year. The recession bottomed out in the last quarter of 1993 and since then the economy has been in a moderate recovery phase. GDP increased by 0.5 per cent in 1994 and by 0.9 per cent in 1995. From the beginning of 1996, the Japanese economy has been recovering

Figure 3. Gross domestic product and gross domestic product per head of the G.7 countries in 1994

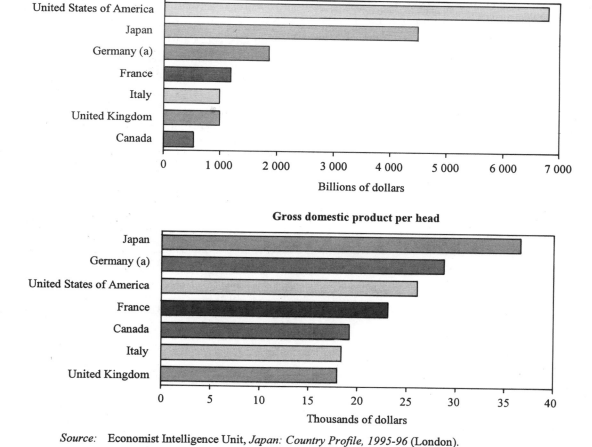

Source: Economist Intelligence Unit, *Japan: Country Profile, 1995-96* (London).

(a) Gross national product.

11

gradually owing to certain promising movements in plant and equipment investment as well as housing construction.

Industry (including manufacturing, mining, construction and utilities) continues to be the dominant economic sector, contributing 40.7 per cent of GDP in 1995 and engaging 35.5 per cent of the employed labour force in 1996. The manufacturing sector is predominated by heavy industries, particularly motor vehicles, steel, machinery, electrical equipment and chemicals. In 1996, Japan was the leading manufacturer of passenger cars, trucks and buses in the world.

The agriculture sector (comprising agriculture, forestry and fishing) contributed only 2.1 per cent of GDP in 1995 and provided employment to 5.1 per cent of the 1996 labour force. The principal crops are rice, potatoes, cabbages, sugar cane, sugar beet and citrus fruits. Farming is generally a family pursuit and there has been only a moderate decrease in the number of farm households despite a swift decline in the number of agricultural workers. Intensive farming practices are common owing to the limited cultivated land area per household. Japan is one of the world's leading fishing nations.

Despite difficulties of terrain, rail transport is highly developed, with over 22,000 km of almost entirely narrow-gauge rail lines. Japan is the leader in the development of high-speed, long-distance passenger rail service. Its road network covers over 1.1 million km, of which about 73 per cent consists of paved roads. For several decades, Japan has ranked among the leading maritime nations of the world. Air transport still constitutes a small share of total domestic transport, but has grown remarkably over the years.

7. Social infrastructure

(a) Education

A kindergarten system provides education for children aged three to five years. In 1995, there were 14,856 kindergarten schools in the country, of which 8,639, or 58.2 per cent, were privately managed, and there were 918,000 male and 891,000 female children enrolled in all kindergarten schools in the country (table 3).

Formal school education starts at the age of six years with free and compulsory six years of elementary education, followed by another three years of compulsory lower or junior secondary education and by a further three years of non-compulsory upper or senior secondary education (see figure 4). Virtually all education at the elementary and lower secondary levels and about 76 per cent at the upper secondary level takes place in public schools (table 3). The upper secondary schools provide three-year courses either in general

Table 3. Educational institutions and students by level of education: 1 May 1995

Type of educational institution	Educational institution				Students (thousands)	
	Total	National	Public	Private	Male	Female
Kindergartens	14 856	49	6 168	8 639	918	891
Elementary schools	24 548	73	24 302	173	4 283	4 088
Lower secondary schools	11 274	78	10 551	645	2 339	2 232
Upper secondary schools	5 501	17	4 164	1 320	2 374	2 351
Technical colleges	62	54	5	3	46	10
Junior colleges	596	36	60	500	43[a]	455[a]
Universities	565	98	52	415	1 725[a]	822[a]
Graduate schools	..	..	..	..	120	33
Special training schools	3 476	152	219	3 105	393	420
Miscellaneous schools	2 821	3	59	2 759	161	160

Source: Ministry of Education.

[a] Including students in advanced courses and short-term courses and part-time students.

Figure 4. The national education system of Japan

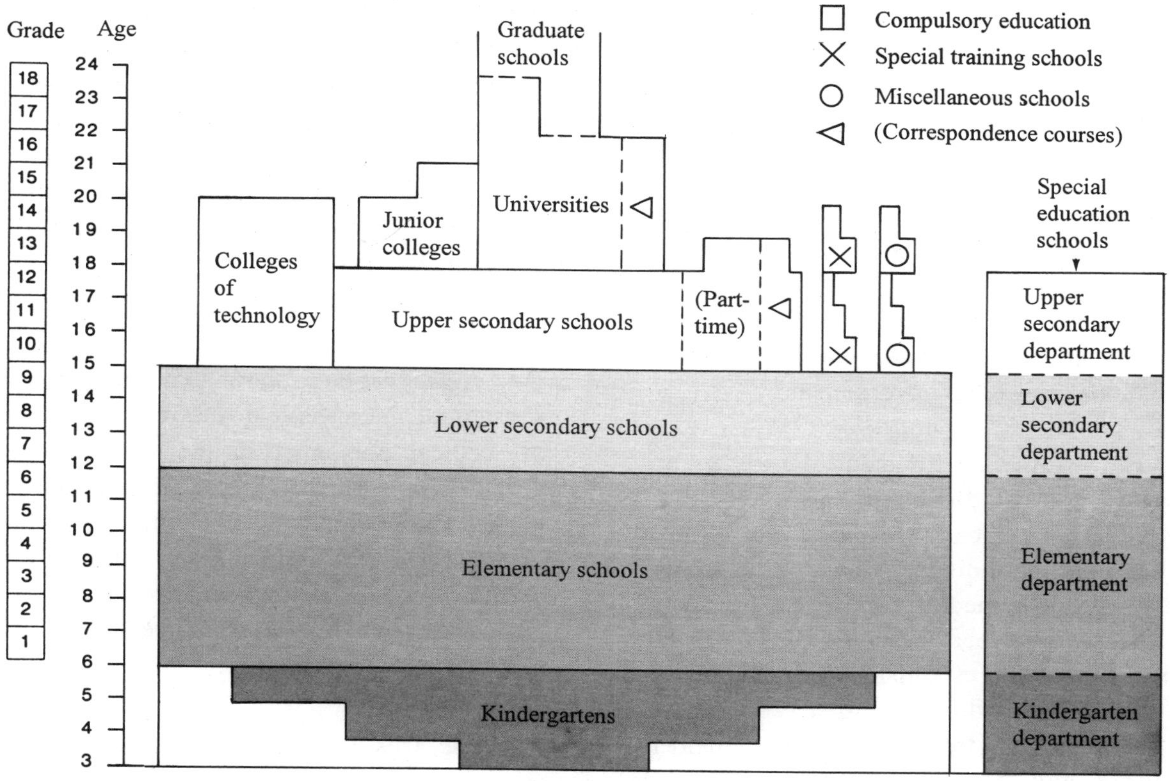

Source: Statistics Bureau, *Statistical Handbook of Japan, 1996* (Tokyo, Government of Japan, 1996).

topics or in vocational subjects such as agriculture, commerce, fine arts and technical studies. Since the 1960s, the proportion of the population aged 15 to 18 years advancing to upper secondary education has been rising rapidly, to reach 96.7 per cent in 1995.

Higher education is provided by three types of institution, universities, junior colleges, and technical colleges. The universities, which are at the top of the education structure, provide four-year courses leading to a bachelor's degree, as well as post-graduate courses. Some universities offer six-year programmes leading to a professional degree. In 1995, Japan had 565 universities (of which 415 or 73 per cent were private) with a combined student enrolment of over 1.7 million male and 822,000 female students (table 3).

Junior colleges, which are mostly private institutions, provide less specialized two-to-three-year courses which mostly emphasize home economics, pedagogy, the humanities or social

sciences. More than 90 per cent of the students in junior colleges are girls; higher education for girls is still being perceived as preparation for marriage or for a short-term career before marriage. Most technical colleges are national institutions established to provide five-year specialized training for technicians in several fields, including the merchant marine.

Tertiary education is also currently provided in 3,476 special training schools, of which 3,105, or 89 per cent, are private institutions. Special training schools offer training in specific skills such as computer science and vocational training, and, in 1995 these institutions enrolled a larger number of women (420,000) compared with men (393,000). Some students attend those schools in addition to attending a university; others enrol to qualify for a technical licence or certificate.

In 1995, there were 2,821 miscellaneous schools, predominantly private, offering a variety of courses in such programmes as medical treatment, education, social welfare, and hygiene, diversifying practical post-secondary training and responding to social and economic demands for certain skills.

(b) Health services

Japan has a well-developed health service infrastructure comprising a network of institutions providing curative medical services and a parallel public health service including screening examinations for particular diseases, prenatal care and infectious disease control provided by the national and local governments.

The institutions for medical care, as designated in the Medical Service Law, are the hospitals and clinics. Hospitals are defined as medical establishments where physicians or dentists provide medical or dental treatment to patients, with a bed capacity of 20 or more, while clinics are establishments with no beds for patients, or with fewer than 20 beds each. As will be noted from table 4, the number of hospitals and clinics as well as beds has increased significantly since 1950.

Generally, Japanese hospitals are closed institutions, in that a private practitioner who refers a patient to a hospital does not have the privilege of extending medical care within the hospital to that patient. Only the staff of the hospital concerned can use the medical equipment and services in that hospital. Group practice among private practitioners is as yet not fully developed; each doctor maintains his or her own independent private clinic.

A long tradition exists in the Japanese industrial community of protecting and assisting employees in their health problems. According to the requirements of the law, an enterprise having more than 50 workers must employ a physician to look after the health of its employees. Many of the large firms in Japan manage their own hospitals and their own insurance groups, and operate health-care programmes and ambulatory care facilities for workers and their families.

Available data show that there have been substantial increases in the various categories of medical personnel in the country over the years. For instance, the number of physicians increased by about 48 per cent, from 154,578 in 1980 to 228,643 in 1994. During the same period, the number of dentists increased from 52,369 to 79,896 and of nurses from 487,169 to 862,013 (table 5).

The fees for medical services are covered by a universal medical insurance system that provides relative equality of access with fees set by a government committee. All residents of Japan are required to have health insurance, and the vast majority are covered by either employees' health insurance or national health insurance. Since 1973, all older persons have been covered by government-sponsored insurance. Patients are free to select the physicians or facilities of their choice. Under the major schemes, the insured pay 10-30 per cent of the medical costs and the remaining portion is borne by the insurance carrier.

Table 4. Number of hospitals, clinics and beds: selected years, 1950 to 1994

Year	Number of hospitals	Number of hospital beds	Number of general clinics	Number of general clinic beds	Number of dental clinics
1950	3 408	275 804	43 827	..	21 380
1960	6 094	686 743	59 008	165 161	27 020
1970	7 974	1 062 553	68 997	249 646	29 911
1980	9 055	1 319 406	77 611	287 835	38 834
1990	10 096	1 687 000	80 852	..	52 216
1994	9 731	1 677 000	85 588	..	57 213

Source: Ministry of Health.

Table 5. Growth in the number of medical personnel by category: 1980-1994

Year	Physicians	Dentists	Pharmacists	Nurses/assistant nurses
1980	154 578	52 369	95 319	487 169
1985	189 531	65 605	114 680	639 936
1990	210 197	73 041	130 604	745 301
1992	218 066	76 343	141 630	795 810
1994	228 643	79 896	157 719	862 013

Source: Ministry of Health.

(c) Housing

Japan has been experiencing serious housing problems over a number of decades caused largely by the effects of three wars, the First World War, the Sino-Japanese War, and the Second World War – with which the country has been directly involved. Successive governments, however, have been conscious of these problems and have been adopting several measures to overcome them. In recent years, there has also been substantial spending on public works designed to rectify the quantitative and qualitative aspects of these problems.

Available data (table 6) indicate that the total number of dwelling units more than doubled, from about 21.1 million in 1963 to about 45.9 million in 1993, but the home-ownership rate appears to have generally declined during this period, from 64.3 per cent in 1963 to 59.8 per cent in 1993. In other words, today only about 60 per cent of the people own the houses in which they live.

Metropolitan land prices are too high for any household to purchase a home for five times its annual income (the stated official objective).

The quality of the housing stock also leaves much to be desired. Although the average floor space per dwelling has increased substantially, from 58.97 square metres in 1963 to 88.38 square metres in 1993, the average floor space per residence is only half that of the United States of America. Around 76 per cent of the dwelling units have flush toilets; thus, the national average conceals the fact that only a fairly low proportion of the households in some rural prefectures have sewage facilities.

Surveys indicate that, for various reasons, Japanese people are generally dissatisfied with their housing conditions and living environment. First, people usually dream of large houses located in a quiet environment and equipped with all modern facilities; but there is a wide gap between their "dream houses" and the ones in which they actually live. Second, they are

Table 6. Housing conditions in Japan: selected years, 1963 to 1993

Year	Number of dwellings (thousands)	House ownership rate (percentage)	Average floor space per dwelling (m²)	Percentage of dwellings with flush toilets
1963	21 090	64.3	59.0	9.2
1968	25 591	60.3	62.5	17.1
1973	31 059	59.2	70.2	31.4
1978	35 451	60.4	75.5	45.9
1983	38 607	62.4	81.6	58.2
1988	42 007	61.3	85.0	66.4
1993	45 879	59.8	88.4	75.6

Source: Statistics Bureau, Management and Coordination Agency.

also conscious of the disparities in housing conditions between their country and developed countries of the West. Third, as noted earlier, the cost of acquiring a house is also unrealistically high in Japan compared with other countries. Fourth, there is also a feeling of widening inequality caused by rapidly rising prices of land surrounding residential areas between those who own land and those who do not. Further, people who had acquired houses earlier enjoy huge benefits, but those who wish to acquire houses now have to pay a very heavy price.

C. WOMEN'S PROFILE

1. Demographic aspects

(a) Gender balance

The changes in the sex composition of the Japanese population based on the census data from 1920 to 1995 are shown in table 7.

It will be noted from table 7 that from 1920 to 1940, males slightly outnumbered females, with the sex ratio (males per 100 females) maintained at a level between 100 and 101. The slight excess of males in the total population during this 20-year period could be attributed largely to a male-favoured sex ratio at birth and higher female than male mortality at practically all ages. The sex ratio declined markedly to 89.0 in 1945 owing to the loss of male population resulting from the overseas deployment of armed forces and the death of soldiers in battle during the Second World War. The repatriation of demobilized soldiers and civilians after the war pushed up the sex ratio to 96.2 in 1950 and since then this ratio has been fluctuating between and 96 and 97. In 1995, there were 95.5 males per 100 females, or 104.7 females for every 100 males, in the country. Thus, the deficit of males created during the Second world War has persisted over the subsequent years, which is mainly attributable to the transition from higher female to higher male mortality during the past 45 years.

The numerical balance between the sexes varies widely across age groups and by residence, as is evident from the relevant data

Table 7. Enumerated population classified by sex, percentage female and gender ratios: censuses of 1920 to 1995

| Census year | Population (thousands) | | | Percentage female | Gender ratio | |
	Both sexes	Male	Female		Males per 100 females	Females per 100 males
1920	55 963	28 044	27 919	49.9	110.4	99.6
1925	59 737	30 013	29 724	49.8	101.0	99.0
1930	64 450	32 390	32 060	49.7	101.0	99.0
1935	69 254	34 734	34 520	49.8	100.6	99.4
1940	73 114	36 566	36 548	50.0	100.0	100.0
1945	71 998	33 894	38 104	52.9	89.0	112.4
1950	84 115	41 241	42 874	51.0	96.2	104.0
1955	90 077	44 243	45 834	50.9	96.5	103.6
1960	94 302	46 300	48 001	50.9	96.5	103.7
1965	99 209	48 692	50 517	50.9	96.4	103.7
1970	104 665	51 369	53 296	50.9	96.4	103.8
1975	111 940	55 091	56 849	50.8	96.9	103.2
1980	117 060	57 594	59 467	50.8	96.9	103.3
1985	121 049	59 497	61 552	50.8	96.7	103.5
1990	123 611	60 697	62 914	50.9	96.5	103.7
1995	125 569	61 341	64 227	51.1	95.5	104.7

Source: Statistics Bureau, Management and coordination Agency, *Japan Statistical Yearbook, 1997* (Tokyo, Government of Japan, 1997).

of the 1990 census presented in table 8. It will be noted that for the country as a whole, males outnumber females at all age groups from 0-4 to 40-44 years, while females outnumber males in the population aged 45 years and over. It will also be noted that the sex ratio decreases gradually from a high of 105.0 at ages 0-4 years with advancing age reaching 100.8 at ages 40-44 years, and at an accelerated pace thereafter to reach 46.6 at very old ages (85 years and over).

An important factor that has contributed to the excess of males over females at the younger ages is the male-favoured sex ratio at birth; in Japan, as in most countries the world over, more male than female babies are born every year. This initial advantage of excess male births is reflected in the relatively high sex ratio (males per 100 females) at ages 0-4 years. The gradual decline of this ratio at subsequent age groups is due to the relatively higher male than female mortality.

The increasing excess of females over males at ages beyond 45 years is due to two factors. First, the current cohort of males and females at these ages are the survivors of those born before the Second World War and the then deaths among those cohorts particularly due to various wars were considerably higher in respect of males than females, resulting in a substantially lower number of males than females at older ages. Further, mortality rates due to other causes are also much higher among males compared with females at the older ages.

There are also significant differences in the age-specific gender ratios between urban and rural areas. While the urban ratios more or less conform to the national pattern noted earlier, in the rural areas an excess of females over males has been reported at ages 20-34 years, reflecting a predominance of males in the rural-to-urban migration streams at these ages.

Table 8. Age-specific gender ratios by residence: 1990 population[a/] census

Age group	Japan		Urban		Rural	
	Males per 100 females	Females per 100 males	Males per 100 females	Females per 100 males	Males per 100 females	Females per 100 males
0-4	105.0	95.2	105.1	95.2	104.8	95.4
5-9	104.9	95.4	104.9	95.3	104.7	95.5
10-14	105.1	95.1	105.1	95.2	105.3	95.0
15-19	104.9	95.4	105.0	95.2	104.3	95.9
20-24	103.1	97.0	104.6	95.6	95.7	104.5
25-29	102.2	96.2	102.9	97.1	98.7	101.3
30-34	101.6	98.4	102.1	97.9	99.9	100.1
35-39	101.0	99.0	100.6	99.4	102.5	97.5
40-44	100.8	99.2	99.6	100.4	105.2	95.1
45-49	98.8	101.2	98.5	101.5	100.1	99.9
50-54	97.7	102.3	98.2	101.8	96.0	104.2
55-59	96.0	104.2	96.6	103.5	94.1	106.3
60-64	92.2	108.4	92.6	108.0	91.4	109.4
65-69	75.5	132.5	75.5	132.5	75.4	132.6
70-74	69.1	144.7	68.9	145.2	69.7	143.6
75-79	65.8	152.1	66.0	151.6	65.2	153.3
80-84	58.8	170.2	58.6	170.5	59.0	169.4
85+	46.6	214.4	46.0	216.7	47.7	209.6
All ages	96.3	103.9	96.9	103.2	94.3	106.1

Source: Statistics Bureau, Management and Coordination Agency.

[a/] Excluding foreign nationals.

(b) Age structure

The age structure, or the distribution of a population by age groups, is the result of past levels and trends of fertility, mortality and migration. The percentage distribution of the population of Japan according to the conventional five-year age groups and sex in 1950, 1970, 1990 and 1995 is given in annex table C.1.

It will be noted from annex table C.1 that the age composition or distribution of the population underwent a very significant transformation during the 45-year period 1950-1995. In 1950, when fertility was still relatively high and mortality low and declining, the highest proportion of the population, among both males and females, was at ages 0-4 years, but the age proportion has been declining gradually with advancing age, reflecting the increasing levels of mortality. Consequently, the age structure of the population assumed the shape of a broad-based pyramid gradually tapering towards the top, typical of countries experiencing high fertility and declining mortality (see figure 5).

Over the years, however, there have been considerable changes in the levels of fertility which, although experiencing a declining trend, were interrupted by a "baby boom" during the period 1971-1974. The declines in both fertility and mortality also did not occur at a uniform

Figure 5. Population pyramid: 1990

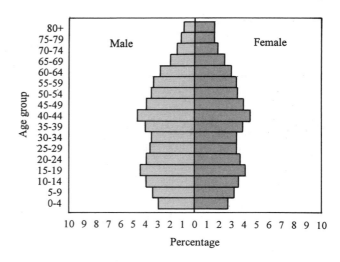

Source: United Nations, *The Sex and Age Distribution of the World Populations: the 1996 Revision* (New York, 1997).

pace over the years. Consequently, there have been very significant shifts in the age-specific proportions and these shifts have in turn resulted in the shape of the age structure changing considerably over the years from the flat-bottomed pyramid of 1950 to the more or less bell-shaped structure of the 1990s. The age structure of the 1994 population (figure 6), with its dents and bulges at appropriate levels, largely reflects the historical changes in the levels and trends in fertility and mortality.

Figure 6. Age structure of the population: 1994

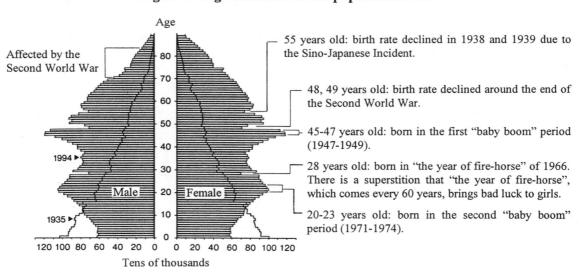

Source: Statistics Bureau, Management and Coordination Agency.

18

The percentage distribution of the 1950, 1970, 1990 and 1995 estimated population of Japan by three broad age groups, that is, 0-14 years comprising children, 15-64 years comprising persons in the working ages, and 65 years and over, or older persons, is given in table 9.

It will be noted from table 9 that in 1950, children aged 0-14 years constituted about 35 per cent of the total population while persons in the working ages 15-64 years accounted for another about 60 per cent and older persons for the remaining 5 per cent, these proportions being slightly different for males and females. With the sharp decline in fertility that has occurred since then, there has been a substantial shrinkage in the relative share of children over the years and the 1995 percentage shares of children were less than half of what they had been in 1950. Concomitantly, there was a rise in the proportionate share of the working-age

population and of older persons, among both males and females, between 1950 and 1995.

The most remarkable change, however, occurred in respect of older persons, whose numbers as well as relative share increased unprecedently between 1950 and 1995 as a consequence of both dramatic declines in fertility and remarkable improvements in mortality. The total number of older persons aged 65 years and over increased more than fourfold, from about 4.1 million in 1950 to about 17.8 million in 1995, while their relative share in the total population rose from 4.9 to 14.2 per cent during the same 45-year period (table 10).

There are three important aspects to the population ageing process in Japan. The first is the rapidity with which this process has been taking place. As will be noted from table 10, a doubling in the proportionate share

Table 9. Percentage distribution of the population by three broad age groups and sex: 1950, 1970, 1990 and 1995

Age group	1950		1970		1990		1995	
	Male	Female	Male	Female	Male	Female	Male	Female
0-14	36.8	34.2	25.0	23.0	19.2	17.6	16.9	15.5
15-64	59.0	60.2	68.7	69.2	70.9	68.3	71.1	68.1
65+	4.2	5.6	6.3	7.8	9.9	14.1	12.0	16.4
Total	100.0	100.0	100.0	100.0	100.0	100.0	100.0	100.0

Source: United Nations, *The Sex and Age Distribution of the World Populations: The 1996 Revision* (New York, 1997).

Table 10. Number and percentage share of older persons (65 years and over) by sex: selected years, 1950 to 2020

Year	Both sexes		Male		Female	
	Number (thou-sands)	Percentage of total popula-tion	Number (thou-sands)	Percentage of total popula-tion	Number (thou-sands)	Percentage of total popula-tion
1950	4 135	4.9	1 737	4.2	2 398	5.6
1970	7 371	7.1	3 236	6.3	4 135	7.8
1990	14 809	12.0	5 964	9.9	8 845	14.1
1995	17 753	14.2	7 338	12.0	10 415	16.4
2000	23 625	18.6	10 103	16.2	13 523	20.9
2020	31 419	25.6	13 716	22.6	17 703	28.0

Source: United Nations, *The Sex and Age Distribution of the World Populations: The 1996 Revision* (New York, 1997).

of the population aged 65 years and over from 7.1 to 14.2 per cent had taken place in Japan within a short span of 25 years (1970-1995), whereas an increase of this magnitude had taken place over a period of around 100 years in most Western industrialized countries. The unprecedently rapid process of population ageing in Japan is due to the fact that, compared with other industrialized countries, the fertility decline in Japan was both the earliest to occur in the post-war period and the greatest in magnitude among them.

The second aspect is related to the first. The current level of population ageing in Japan is not yet as high as in many of the Western industrialized countries. But given the current pace at which the process is occurring in Japan, it is likely that the relative share of older persons will be even higher than the current levels of other industrialized countries within the next few decades. Recent projections prepared by the United Nations indicate that the pace of population ageing in Japan will increase at an accelerating speed in the twenty-first century and that by 2020, nearly 26 per cent of the population, or one in every four Japanese people, will be aged 65 years or more (table 10).

Third, population ageing is more pronounced among women than among men in Japan. In absolute as well as relative terms, there have always been more older women than older men

in the country. In 1995, for example, women constituted 58.7 per cent of the total population aged 65 years and over, and 16.4 per cent among all females compared with 12.0 per cent among males were senior citizens in that year. Projections also indicate that this gender disparity will continue during the next few decades, and that by 2020 women will account for about 56 per cent of all older persons and 28 per cent of all females in the country, the corresponding relative share among males being about 23 per cent (table 10).

(c) Marital status

The numerical distribution of persons aged 15 years and over by marital status and sex is given in annex table C.2, and the corresponding percentage distribution in text table 11.

It will be noted from table 11 that the proportion remaining single or unmarried among persons aged 15 years and over has been increasing since 1985 for both males and females, and that in all years for which data are given in the table, these proportions have been significantly higher among males than among females. The percentage reported as married has also been declining since 1980 and these proportions have also been consistently higher for males than for females.

However, the proportions living in a state of marital disruption, that is, either widowed

Table 11. Percentage distribution of persons aged 15 years and over by marital status and sex: census years, 1960 to 1995

Year	Single		Married		Widowed		Divorced		Total[a]	
	Male	Female	Male	Female	Male	Female	Male	Female	Male	Female
1960	34.8	26.9	60.8	56.8	3.2	14.1	0.9	2.1	100.0	100.0
1965	34.5	27.1	61.7	56.9	3.0	13.1	0.8	1.9	100.0	100.0
1970	32.3	24.9	64.2	60.3	2.7	12.8	0.8	2.0	100.0	100.0
1975	29.2	21.5	67.4	63.7	2.6	12.7	0.9	2.1	100.0	100.0
1980	28.5	20.9	67.6	64.0	2.4	12.4	1.2	2.5	100.0	100.0
1985	29.6	21.7	66.2	62.5	2.4	12.7	1.6	3.0	100.0	100.0
1990	31.2	23.4	63.8	60.3	2.4	12.3	1.8	3.2	100.0	100.0
1995	31.8	24.0	62.7	58.9	2.6	13.0	2.2	3.7	100.0	100.0

Source: Statistics Bureau, Management and Coordination Agency.

[a] Including marital status not reported.

or divorced, were higher for females than for males in all census years from 1960 to 1995. In particular, the proportion widowed among females was about four to five times higher than among males. For instance, in 1995, the proportion widowed among females (13.0 per cent) was five times higher than the proportion of 2.6 per cent among males. The considerably higher incidence of widowhood among females compared with males is due to several factors. First, as has been noted earlier, mortality among males is higher than among females, and this, together with the fact that Japanese women usually marry men at least a few years their senior, results in a higher incidence of widowhood among women. Second, an equally important reason is that widowed men have a better chance of remarrying than widowed women and thus ending their widowhood.

2. Educational background

(a) First-level education

The 1946 Constitution of Japan contains declarations on the universal right to education. The Fundamental Law on Education enacted in 1947 upholds the principle of equal accessibility to education according to individual ability; prohibits sexual discrimination in education; and lays down the principle of co-education. Consequently, as noted in section B of this profile,

the six-year programme of first-level or elementary education is free and compulsory for all Japanese children aged between 6 and 11 years.

The number of students enrolled in elementary schools from 1945 to 1994 is shown in table 12. It will be noted from this table that the number of students enrolled in elementary schools fluctuated between 1945 and 1994, recording an increase between 1945 and 1960, a decline between 1960 and 1970, a rise between 1970 and 1980, and thereafter a gradual decline until 1994.

The fluctuations in elementary-level enrolments noted in the preceding paragraph reflect the changing levels and trends in fertility over the years. The significant increase in enrolments between 1945 and 1960 was due to the baby boom in the immediate post-war years 1947-1949. The decrease in enrolments between 1960 and 1970, in spite of free and compulsory education, was due to the decrease in absolute numbers of births after the baby boom. The increase in enrolments between 1970 and 1980 is accounted for by the fact that since the mid-1960s, the absolute number of births has been increasing, resulting in a corresponding increase in the population of school-going age in the 1970s. The sharp reduction is fertility during the 1970s and 1980 led to a decline in

Table 12. Growth in elementary school enrolments by sex: 1945 to 1994

Year	Number of pupils enrolled (thousands)			Percentage of total enrolments	
	Both sexes	Male	Female	Male	Female
1945	10 635	5 373	5 262	50.5	49.5
1950	11 191	5 667	5 524	50.6	59.4
1955	12 267	6 241	6 026	50.9	49.1
1960	12 591	6 425	6 166	51.0	49.0
1965	9 876	5 019	4 857	50.8	49.2
1970	9 558	4 852	4 706	50.8	49.2
1975	10 365	5 308	5 057	51.2	48.8
1980	11 827	6 062	5 765	51.3	48.7
1985	11 095	5 682	5 413	51.2	48.8
1990	9 373	4 798	4 575	51.2	48.8
1993	8 789	4 506	4 283	51.3	48.7
1994	8 583	4 391	4 192	51.2	48.8

Sources: ESCAP, *Population of Japan*, Country Monograph Series No. 11 (New York, 1984); and UNESCO, *Statistical Yearbook*, 1988, 1995 and 1996.

the absolute number of children of school-going age in the late 1980s and the early 1990s.

It will also be noted from table 12 that the relative share of girls in total elementary-level enrolments has consistently been less than 50 per cent. This gender disparity is due to the fact that, as noted earlier in this section (table 8), there are fewer females than males in the appropriate age groups. However, relevant data indicate that the enrolment ratio at this level is 100 per cent for both boys and girls (table 13).

(b) Secondary-level education

As noted earlier, the second-level education in Japan consists of three-year lower secondary schooling which is free and compulsory, and another three-year non-compulsory, upper-secondary programme. Data from the Ministry of Education indicate that the total number of

pupils in the lower-secondary stream fluctuated between 1955 and 1995, reflecting changes in the size of the relevant age cohorts owing to past shifts in fertility trends. It is also evident from table 14 that the number of girls enrolled at the lower-secondary level has been considerably lower than the number of male students. This gender disparity in enrolments has been due to the fact that males have consistently outnumbered females at ages 10-14 years, the age cohort relevant to lower secondary-level enrolments.

Although education at the upper-secondary level is not free and compulsory, an increasing proportion of male and female students have been advancing from lower-secondary to upper-secondary levels over the years. Estimates based on the data from the School Basic Survey conducted annually by the Ministry of Education since 1948 indicate that the advancement rate from lower-secondary to

Table 13. Elementary school enrolment ratios by sex: 1975 to 1994

Year	Gross enrolment ratio			Net enrolment ratio		
	Both sexes	Male	Female	Both sexes	Male	Female
1975	99	99	100	99	99	100
1980	101	101	101	100	100	100
1985	102	102	102	100	100	100
1990	100	100	100	100	100	100
1994	102	102	102	100	100	100

Source: UNESCO, *Statistical Yearbook* (various years).

Table 14. Enrolments in lower-secondary schools by sex: 1955 to 1995

Year	Number of pupils enrolled (thousands)			Percentage of total enrolments	
	Both sexes	Male	Female	Male	Female
1955	5 884	2 981	2 903	50.7	49.3
1960	5 900	3 009	2 891	51.0	49.0
1965	5 957	3 059	2 898	51.4	48.6
1970	4 717	2 409	2 308	51.1	48.9
1975	4 762	2 435	2 327	51.1	48.9
1980	5 094	2 607	2 487	51.2	48.8
1985	5 990	3 068	2 922	51.2	48.8
1990	5 369	2 748	2 621	51.2	48.8
1995	4 570	2 339	2 231	51.2	48.8

Source: Ministry of Education, *School Basic Survey* (various years).

upper-secondary level increased from 48.0 per cent in 1950 to 94.2 per cent in 1993 for boys, and from 36.7 to 96.5 per cent for girls, during the same period (table 15).

Table 15. Advancement ratio from lower-secondary to upper-secondary school: 1950 to 1993

| Year | Advancement rate (percentage) | |
	Male	Female
1950	48.0	36.7
1955	55.5	47.4
1960	59.6	55.9
1965	71.7	69.6
1970	81.6	82.7
1975	91.3	93.0
1980	93.1	95.4
1985	92.8	94.9
1993	94.2	96.5

Source: Ministry of Education, *School Basic Survey.*

As noted in section B above, upper-secondary schools offer general education and specialized education. The courses of study in the second category include agriculture, industry, commerce, fishery, home economics, nursing, science, mathematics and English language. In 1994, a decision was made to establish integrated courses that allow students to select both general education and specialized education (integrated courses). Upper-secondary schools with part-time courses and correspondence courses are also available to those young people who want to study while working to obtain an upper-secondary education.

According to data from the School Basic Survey of the Ministry of Education, total enrolments in all types of upper-secondary schools had increased by about 82 per cent from about 2.6 million in 1955 to 4.7 million in 1995, but this increase had been more pronounced in the case of female students than male students. While the enrolment of boys in upper-secondary schools increased by about 59 per cent, that of girls more than doubled during the 40-year period. Consequently, the relative share of females in total upper-secondary enrolments increased from 42.4 per cent in 1995 to 49.8 per cent in 1995 (table 16).

Enrolment ratios are not available separately for lower-secondary and upper-secondary levels. However, the ratios for both levels combined indicate an increase in these ratios among males as well as females between 1975 and 1994, and that in 1994 nearly 98 per cent of all males and 99 per cent of all females aged 12-17 years were enrolled in secondary schools (table 17).

As noted earlier, since 1994, the upper-secondary school is divided into three streams: general education stream; specialized or vocational education stream; and integrated stream. The numerical and percentage distribution of the students enrolled in full-day courses of the

Table 16. Enrolments in upper-secondary schools by sex: 1955 to 1995

| Year | Pupil enrolments (thousands) | | | Percentage of total enrolments | |
	Both sexes	Male	Female	Male	Female
1955	2 592	1 497	1 095	57.8	42.2
1960	3 239	1 756	1 483	54.2	45.8
1965	5 074	2 661	2 413	52.4	47.6
1970	4 232	2 153	2 079	50.9	49.1
1975	4 333	2 185	2 148	50.4	49.6
1980	4 622	2 330	2 292	50.4	49.6
1985	5 178	2 609	2 569	50.4	49.6
1990	5 623	2 830	2 793	50.3	49.7
1995	4 725	2 374	2 351	50.2	49.8

Source: Ministry of Education, *School Basic Survey* (various years).

Table 17. Secondary school enrolment ratios by sex: 1975 to 1994

Year	Gross enrolment ratio			Net enrolment ratio		
	Both sexes	Male	Female	Both sexes	Male	Female
1975	92	91	92	..	..	..
1980	93	92	94	93	92	94
1985	96	95	97	96	..	..
1990	97	96	98	97	..	..
1994	98	98	99	..	..	..

Source: UNESCO, *Statistical Yearbook,* 1988 and 1996.

upper-secondary level in 1995 by the three streams and by various vocational courses is given in table 18. It will be noted that roughly three fourths (74.2 per cent) of all students are enrolled in the general education stream, but this proportion among females (76.6 per cent) is significantly higher than among males (71.8 per cent). The proportion enrolled in the vocational stream is higher among males (28.1 per cent) compared with females (23.3 per cent). Only 0.1 per cent among male as well as female students are enrolled in the integrated stream.

It will also be noted from table 18 that in respect of those opting for specialized or vocational studies, the largest proportion among male students are enrolled in technical courses (16.1 per cent) and the second largest in commerce (6.1 per cent), while among females, the preferred field of study is commerce (13.0 per cent), followed by home economics (3.7 per cent). It is thus evident that there is a strong tendency for students to pursue fields of study conforming to socially defined feminine and masculine roles.

(c) Tertiary education

The institutions of tertiary or higher education in Japan include junior colleges, colleges of technologies, universities and special training colleges. These four types of institutions differ

Table 18. Numerical and percentage distribution of upper-secondary school enrolments[a] by type of course and sex: 1995

Stream/study course	Both sexes		Male		Female	
	Number (thousands)	Percentage	Number (thousands)	Percentage	Number (thousands)	Percentage
General education stream	**3 499.0**	**74.2**	**1 702.0**	**71.8**	**1 797.0**	**76.6**
Vocational educational stream:	**1 212.9**	**25.7**	**665.9**	**28.1**	**547.0**	**23.3**
Agriculture	132.8	2.8	87.9	3.7	44.9	1.9
Technical	415.0	8.8	382.0	16.1	33.0	1.4
Commerce	450.0	9.5	143.8	6.1	306.2	13.0
Fishery	13.0	0.3	11.0	0.5	2.0	0.1
Home economics	90.7	1.9	4.7	0.2	86.0	3.7
Nursing	24.0	0.5	0.3	–	23.7	1.0
Other	87.4	1.9	36.2	1.5	51.2	2.2
Integrated educational stream	**5.5**	**0.1**	**2.6**	**0.1**	**2.9**	**0.1**
Total	**4 717.4**	**100.0**	**2 370.5**	**100.0**	**2 346.9**	**100.0**

Source: Ministry of Education, *School Basic Survey,* 1995.

[a] Including only enrolments in full-day courses.

in regard to curricula, period of instruction and their links to secondary education.

Junior colleges provide a thorough liberal arts education in specialized areas of study via research and instruction, and the courses are designed to develop the necessary abilities for employment and life after college. The number of years required to complete the courses is two to three, after which students receive an associate degree.

The distribution of student enrolments in junior colleges by sex from 1955 to 1995 is shown in table 19. It will be noted that in all years, females have consistently outnumbered males in total enrolments and that the relative share of male students has been declining while that of female students has been increasing. In 1995, nearly 91 per cent of the students in junior colleges were females.

Data relating to the fields of study pursued by students enrolled in regular courses at junior colleges analysed in table 20 show that in 1995, while the majority of female students (53.7 per cent) were enrolled in arts-based courses such as humanities and home economics, the majority of male students (50.4 per cent) were enrolled in science-based professional courses such as engineering, agriculture and health sciences. These enrolment patterns

Table 19. Distribution of student enrolments in junior colleges by sex: selected years, 1955 to 1995

| Year | Student enrolments (thousands) | | | Percentage of total enrolments | |
	Both sexes	Male	Female	Male	Female
1955	78	36	42	46.2	53.8
1960	83	27	56	32.5	67.5
1965	148	38	110	25.7	74.3
1970	263	45	218	17.1	82.9
1975	354	49	305	13.8	86.2
1980	371	41	330	11.1	88.9
1985	371	38	333	10.2	89.8
1990	479	41	438	8.6	91.4
1995	499	44	455	8.8	91.2

Source: Ministry of Education, *School Basic Survey* (various years).

Table 20. Distribution of students enrolled in regular courses at junior colleges by major field of study and sex: 1995

| Major field of study | Both sexes | | Males | | Females | |
	Number	Percentage	Number	Percentage	Number	Percentage
Humanities	129 176	26.4	3 233	7.7	125 943	28.1
Social sciences	65 363	13.4	13 464	32.1	51 899	11.6
Liberal arts	17 224	3.5	195	0.5	17 029	3.8
Engineering	22 360	4.6	16 374	39.1	5 986	1.3
Agriculture	3 692	0.8	1 951	4.7	1 741	0.4
Health science	30 651	6.3	2 766	6.6	27 885	6.2
Home economics	115 477	23.6	886	2.1	114 591	25.6
Education	74 381	15.2	838	2.0	73 543	16.4
Arts	22 759	4.7	2 150	5.1	20 609	4.6
Other	8 239	1.7	33	0.1	8 206	1.8
All courses	489 322	100.0	41 890	100.0	447 432	100.0

Source: Ministry of Education, *School Basic Survey,* 1 May 1995.

confirm the tendency for sex-stereotyping in regard to the selection of study areas noted earlier in respect of upper-secondary education.

Colleges of technology are different from universities and junior colleges in that they accommodate lower secondary-school graduates. These institutions offer courses in specialized areas of study which are designed to develop vocational and technological abilities. It takes a minimum of five years to complete course work, and technology college graduates are eligible to apply for admission to a university.

Enrolment data by sex indicate that the vast majority of students enrolled in colleges of technology are males. Although there has been a spectacular increase in female enrolments in both absolute and relative terms since 1970, females accounted for only about 18 per cent of the total enrolments in the colleges of technology in 1995 (table 21).

In Japan, the universities are intended to provide a wide range of knowledge with a focus on learning, and comprehensive education in specialized areas of study through research and instruction. Only upper-secondary school graduates, or those with better academic ability are eligible for admission to universities, which confer bachelor's degrees upon completion of a minimum of a four-year course of study, but six years in the case of medicine, dentistry and veterinary medicine. Universities also have graduate schools which provide courses leading to master's and doctor's degrees upon completion of the requisite number of years of study.

Data from the School Basic Surveys indicate that total student enrolments in the universities had increased almost fivefold from 523,000 in 1955 to about 2.5 million in 1995, but this increase was more pronounced in the case of female than male enrolments. Whereas the number of male students increased almost fourfold from about 458,000 in 1955 to about 1.7 million in 1995, the number of female students increased almost 13-fold, from about 65,000 to 822,000 during the same 40-year period. Consequently, the relative share of females in total university enrolments rose from 12.4 per cent in 1944 to 32.3 per cent in 1995. Despite this enormous increase, women continue to be very much under-represented in university education (table 22).

Data from the 1995 School Basic Survey show that the most popular field of studies for females at the undergraduate level in the universities is humanities, followed by social sciences, education and health. The proportions among female students enrolled in such courses were higher than the corresponding proportions for male students. Considerably larger proportions among males were, however, enrolled in social sciences and engineering and natural science courses (table 23).

The distribution of students enrolled in special training colleges or professional training colleges with advanced courses is given in table 24. It will be noted from this table that the number of students enrolled in special training colleges had almost doubled from about 433,000 to about 813,000 in 1995.

Table 21. Student enrolments in colleges of technology by sex: selected years, 1970 to 1995

Year	Number of students enrolled			Percentage of total enrolments	
	Both sexes	Male	Female	Male	Female
1970	44 314	43 641	673	98.5	1.5
1975	47 955	47 219	736	98.5	1.5
1980	46 348	45 431	917	98.0	2.0
1985	48 288	46 565	1 723	96.4	3.6
1990	52 930	48 253	4 677	91.2	8.8
1995	56 234	46 268	9 966	82.3	17.7

Source: Ministry of Education.

Table 22. University enrolments by sex: selected years, 1955 to 1995

Year	Number of students enrolled (thousands)			Percentage of total enrolments	
	Both sexes	Male	Female	Male	Female
1955	523	458	65	87.6	12.4
1960	626	540	86	86.3	13.7
1965	938	785	153	83.7	16.3
1970	1 407	1 154	253	82.0	18.0
1975	1 734	1 366	368	78.8	21.2
1980	1 835	1 430	405	77.9	22.1
1985	1 849	1 414	435	76.5	23.5
1990	2 133	1 549	584	72.6	27.4
1995	2 547	1 725	822	67.7	32.3

Source: Ministry of Education, *School Basic Survey* (various years).

Table 23. University enrolments by major field of study and sex: 1995

Major study field	Both sexes		Male		Female	
	Number	Percentage	Number	Percentage	Number	Percentage
Humanities	374 964	16.1	123 907	7.9	251 057	32.7
Social sciences	933 624	40.1	733 987	47.0	199 637	26.0
Natural sciences	82 764	3.6	63 254	4.0	19 510	2.5
Engineering	456 707	19.6	421 379	27.0	35 328	4.6
Agriculture	71 880	3.1	46 528	3.0	25 352	3.3
Health	122 081	5.2	64 507	4.1	57 574	7.5
Home economics	40 803	1.8	1 186	0.1	39 617	5.2
Education	147 253	6.3	62 725	4.0	84 528	11.0
Arts	59 607	2.6	19 868	1.3	39 739	5.2
Other	41 148	1.8	25 604	1.6	15 544	2.0
Total	2 330 831	100.0	1 562 945	100.0	767 886	100.0

Source: Ministry of Education, *School Basic Survey, 1995.*

Table 24. Enrolments in special training colleges by sex: 1980 to 1995

Year	Both sexes		Male		Female	
	Number (thousands)	Percentage	Number (thousands)	Percentage	Number (thousands)	Percentage
1980	433	100.0	145	33.5	288	66.5
1985	538	100.0	226	42.0	312	58.0
1990	791	100.0	380	48.0	411	52.0
1995	813	100.0	393	48.3	420	51.7

Source: Ministry of Education, *School Basic Survey* (various years).

However, this increase was more pronounced in the case of males compared with females. Consequently, the relative share of males in total enrolments increased from 33.5 per cent in 1980 to 48.3 per cent in 1995, while that of females declined from 66.5 to 57.7 per cent during the same 15-year period. Nevertheless, women have consistently outnumbered males in total enrolments in special training colleges.

Although enrolments in various institutions of higher or tertiary-level education have been increasing over the years, estimates indicate that less than a third of all persons aged 20-24 years were enrolled in these institutions in 1990. This ratio was considerably higher for males, at 35.1 per cent, compared with females, at 22.9 per cent (table 25).

Available data also indicate that while the enrolment ratios are about the same for males and females at the first and second levels of education, the male ratio is considerably higher than the female ratio at the third level of education (figure 7).

Figure 7. Enrolment ratios by level of education and sex: 1991

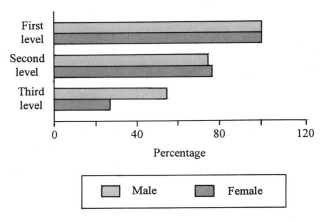

Source: Statistics Bureau, *Statistical Handbook of Japan, 1996* (Tokyo, Government of Japan, 1996).

Table 25. Gross enrolment ratios in third-level education by sex: selected years, 1975 to 1990

Year	Both sexes	Male	Female
1975	24.6	33.0	16.0
1980	30.5	40.4	20.3
1985	27.8	35.5	19.8
1990	29.1	35.1	22.9

Source: UNESCO, *Statistical Yearbook,* 1988 and 1996.

(d) Teachers

In Japan, women have been participating increasingly in the education process, not only as students or learners but also as teachers or instructors. Data from the School Basic Surveys conducted annually by the Ministry of Education show that since 1955 the number of female teachers has been increasing in absolute as well as relative terms at all levels of the educational institutions (annex table C.3 and text table 26).

Table 26. Female teachers as a percentage of all teachers in various levels of education: selected years, 1955 to 1995

Year	Elementary schools	Lower secondary schools	Upper secondary schools	Junior colleges	Technical colleges	Universities
1955	46.5	22.9	17.6	19.0	–	4.7
1960	45.3	21.7	17.1	22.6	–	5.5
1965	48.4	25.3	17.2	25.6	–	6.7
1970	49.1	26.5	16.7	29.2	1.2	7.8
1975	54.8	29.4	17.0	30.4	1.6	8.3
1980	56.6	32.0	17.9	34.0	2.0	9.5
1985	56.0	33.9	18.7	34.1	2.5	9.9
1990	58.3	36.4	20.5	34.4	3.5	11.5
1995	61.2	39.2	23.2	36.6	4.9	13.6

Source: Ministry of Education, *School Basic Survey* (various years).

In 1995, women constituted the majority, 61.2 per cent, of all elementary school teachers, their relative share having increased steadily from 46.5 per cent in 1955. However, in the lower-secondary and upper-secondary schools, women accounted for only 39.2 and 23.2 per cent of the total teachers at these levels respectively in 1995. Although, as noted earlier, the majority of the students in junior colleges are women, the majority of teachers are men; only about 37 per cent of all junior college teachers in 1995 were females, this proportion having risen steadily from 19.0 per cent in 1955. Women are very much under-represented in the faculties of technical colleges and universities, constituting about 5 per cent of the teaching staff in technical colleges and about 14 per cent in universities in 1995.

(e) Educational attainment

Consequent upon the increasing participation of males and females in the education process, the level of educational attainment of the population has been rising over the years. Available data indicate that the proportion of females aged 25 years and over with no schooling had decreased from 0.6 per cent in 1980 to 0.0 per cent in 1990, while those with secondary-level education increased from 42.1 to 47.3 per cent during the decade. The most spectacular increase has been recorded in respect of females aged 25 years with post-secondary education: this proportion rose from 9.7 per cent in 1980 to 16.7 per cent in 1990. There are also significant differences in the level of educational attainment between rural

and urban women. For instance, the proportion of women with post-secondary education in urban areas (18.9 per cent) was almost twice the corresponding proportion of 9.7 per cent reported in respect of rural women in 1995 (table 27).

The highest level of education attained also varies according to age, with the proportion completing secondary education declining with advancing age. For instance, in 1995, nearly 42 per cent of women aged 25-34 years had post-secondary education, compared with about 3.5 per cent among older women aged 65 years and over, reflecting the historical trends in levels of educational participation. At each age group, the proportion with post-secondary education was significantly higher in urban compared with rural areas (annex table C.4).

3. Health status

(a) Background

As noted above in section B, industrialization and modernization have resulted in tremendous improvements in living standards and in the health status of Japanese men and women over the past several decades. The development and expansion of modern public health and medical care services led to sharp declines in the incidence of morbidity and mortality. The general health status of the people of Japan is comparable with that obtaining in other highly industrialized countries.

Table 27. Percentage distribution of the population aged 25 years and over by educational attainment and sex: 1980 and 1990

Highest educational level attained	1980 Japan		1990 Japan		1990 Urban areas		1990 Rural areas	
	Both sexes	Female	Both sexes	Female	Both sexes	Female	Both sexes	Female
No schooling	0.4	0.6	–	–	–	–	–	–
First-level	45.3	47.6	34.3	36.0	30.2	32.2	47.5	47.8
Second-level	39.7	42.1	44.5	47.3	45.9	48.9	40.0	42.5
Post-secondary	14.6	9.7	21.2	16.7	23.9	18.9	12.5	9.7
Total	100.0	100.0	100.0	100.0	100.0	100.0	100.0	100.0

Source: UNESCO, *Statistical Yearbook*, 1988 and 1995.

Since the early part of this century, the Japanese Government has been implementing special measures to protect the health of women and children. The maternal and child health administration started with the launching in 1916 of field surveys on the state of maternal and child health. Subsequently, the establishment of hospitals and nursing homes and house calls by midwives gradually became widespread. With the enactment of the Public Health Act in 1937, maternal and child health administration became involved in the prevention of tuberculosis. The distribution of a maternal health passbook in 1942 marked the beginning of a registration system for pregnant women.

Under the terms of the 1947 Child Welfare Law and the 1948 Decision on the Guidelines of Measures on Maternal and Child Health, several measures, such as health instructions and medical check-ups, were implemented. Since the enactment of the Maternal and Child Health Act in 1965, maternal and child health activities have been carried out in an integrated manner covering the adolescent period, pregnancy, childbirth and child care, with focus on protection and respect for motherhood and maintenance and improvement of infant and child health. The Government also encouraged the establishment of private organizations and volunteer groups to actively participate in and promote maternal and child health activities.

The issuance of the Female Health Promotion Policy in 1978 underscores the Government's commitment to further enhance the health status of women and children. The components of this policy include health examinations for women, community-based programmes for nutritional development and workshops for women leaders. Increasing opportunities have been provided to women for consultation and health guidance in regard to pregnancy, childbirth and child care, in addition to health examinations for pregnant women and nursing mothers through regular home visits. Improvements have been made in medical facilities to ensure safer delivery of babies.

Under the provisions of the Working Women's Welfare Law, employers are required to grant their women employees leave to receive medical check-ups and arrange for shorter working hours to reduce their physical burdens. The Women's and Young Workers' Office in every prefecture now has a Medical Advisor for Maternal health to counsel employers and working women. Furthermore, enterprises have been officially encouraged to appoint "Promoters of Maternal Health". The medical security system of Japan includes maternity allowances, delivery expenses, nursing allowances and maternal benefits.

Under the provisions of the Labour Standard Law, working mothers are entitled to six weeks leave before and after childbirth, as well as leave for child care. Restrictions also exist on overtime work, employment during holidays and at night, and work deemed hazardous or harmful. The Working Women's Welfare Law entitles working mothers of infants to take leave for a specified period in order to take care of them.

In 1978, the Government initiated a medical check-up programme to assess the health of women engaged in family occupations. The findings have formed the basis for the development of regional projects for the health maintenance of such women, focusing on nutrition. As part of these activities, 150,000 women volunteers have been trained to become community leaders in nutrition development.

(b) Morbidity

Over the decades, the morbidity pattern has undergone drastic changes in Japan. Until 1950, tuberculosis was widely prevalent in the country, being a major cause of morbidity as well as mortality, particularly among young persons. Since 1950, however, the incidence of tuberculosis has been drastically reduced through the development of superior medical technology and a programme of extensive testing and vaccination. Today, tuberculosis is hardly a cause of death and affects only a few older people.

The years immediately following the Second World War witnessed a large number of cases of typhus and other contagious diseases, their incidence being largely due to mass repatriation from overseas and the confused social conditions then prevalent in the country. However, with improvements in the socio-economic situation and in public health administration, there has been a sharp decline in contagious diseases. Today, cholera has been completely eradicated; typhus has become almost non-existent; diphtheria and contagious meningitis, and myelitis, have decreased considerably, while cases of typhoid and dysentery are very rare.

Nevertheless, Japan is today facing a range of health problems. The changing lifestyles of Japanese people resulting from rising living standards have led to the growing importance of non-communicable diseases. There has been an increase in the incidence of apoplexy, high blood pressure, heart ailments, mental disorders etc. resulting from fatigue and physical and mental tensions, as well as in the incidence of cancer. These "diseases of civilization" now constitute the major causes of mortality in the country (see figure 8).

In recent years, the Government has been concerned about the worldwide epidemic of acquired immune deficiency syndrome (AIDS). The first confirmed case of AIDS in Japan was reported in 1985; by 1989, there were 108 confirmed cases and between 1,000 and 2,500 others infected with the virus. Officials anticipated a fourfold increase by 1992, and the Government enacted the Law Concerning the Prevention of Acquired Immune Deficiency Syndrome, which came into force in February 1989. According to data from the Ministry of Health, in December 1993 there was a total of 1,271 reported cases of human immune deficiency virus (HIV) patients and carriers, of whom 617, or about 49 per cent, were women. These data also indicated that about 75 per cent of all HIV patients and carriers were aged 20-29 years, while another about 12 per cent were below 20 years of age. On the other hand, nearly 71 per cent of the 654 males reported to be infected with HIV were over 30 years old (table 28).

(c) Mortality

As a result of the rapid economic development, improvement in living standards and the progress made in regard to medical technology, including improved environmental sanitation, there have been remarkable declines in mortality rates over the past several decades. The crude death rate, which stood at 18.2 per thousand in 1930, declined to 11.0 per thousand in 1950 and thereafter declined gradually to reach an estimated 7.5 in 1995.

Figure 8. Death rates by major causes: 1950 to 1994

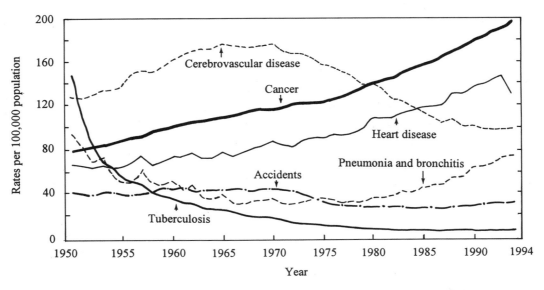

Source: Statistics Bureau, *Statistical Handbook of Japan, 1996* (Tokyo, Government of Japan, 1996).

31

Table 28. Reported cases of HIV/AIDS patients and carriers by age group and sex as at December 1993

Age group (years)	Both sexes		Male		Female	
	Number	Percentage	Number	Percentage	Number	Percentage
Under 20	85	6.7	9	1.4	76	12.3
20-29	642	50.5	180	27.5	462	74.9
30-39	273	21.5	218	33.3	55	8.9
40-49	173	13.6	159	24.3	14	2.3
50+	93	7.3	88	13.5	5	0.8
Age unknown	5	0.4	–	–	5	0.8
Total	1 271	100.0	654	100.0	617	100.0

Source: Ministry of Health.

Together with the decline in general death rates, there have also been marked declines in infant mortality and maternal mortality rates. Estimates indicate that the infant mortality rate declined from 84 per thousand live births in 1940 to 60 in 1950 and further to 13 in 1970 and to about 4.5 in 1992. The infant mortality rate of 4 per thousand live births during the period 1990-1995 is among the lowest in the world. The perinatal death rate, estimated at 5.2 per thousand live births in 1992, is also at a low level internationally.

The maternal mortality rate, estimated at 240 per hundred thousand live births in 1940, declined to 20.5 in 1980 and further to 9.2 in 1992. The current rate, though very low compared with other Asian countries, is nevertheless high compared with rates obtaining in Western European countries and the United States.

The age-specific death rates for selected years from 1970 to 1994 given in annex table C.5 show that mortality rates declined at all ages between 1970 and 1994, and that, by and large, these declines were more pronounced at younger ages compared with the older age cohorts. It is also evident from this table that the mortality rates for females were lower than the corresponding male rates at all ages, but that this gender disparity generally widened with advancing age.

The progress made in regard to the reduction in mortality rates is also reflected in the increase in the life expectancy of Japanese people. Estimates prepared by the Ministry of Health and Welfare indicate that life expectancy at birth for females increased from 62.75 years in 1955 to 82.98 years in 1994, or by about 20 years in 39 years, the corresponding increase for males being from 63.60 to 76.57 years, or by about 13 years, during the same period. (Today, a Japanese female can expect to live, on the average, 6.41 years longer than a Japanese male (table 29)). Japan also has the highest average longevity in the world (figure 9).

Table 29. Expectation of life at birth by sex: 1955 to 1994

(Years)

Year	Male	Female	Female/male difference
1955	63.60	67.75	4.15
1965	67.74	72.92	5.18
1970	69.31	74.66	5.35
1975	71.73	76.89	5.16
1980	73.35	78.76	5.41
1985	74.78	80.48	5.70
1990	75.92	81.90	5.98
1994	76.57	82.98	6.41

Source: Ministry of Health and Welfare.

Figure 9. Life expectancy at birth: Japan and other selected countries

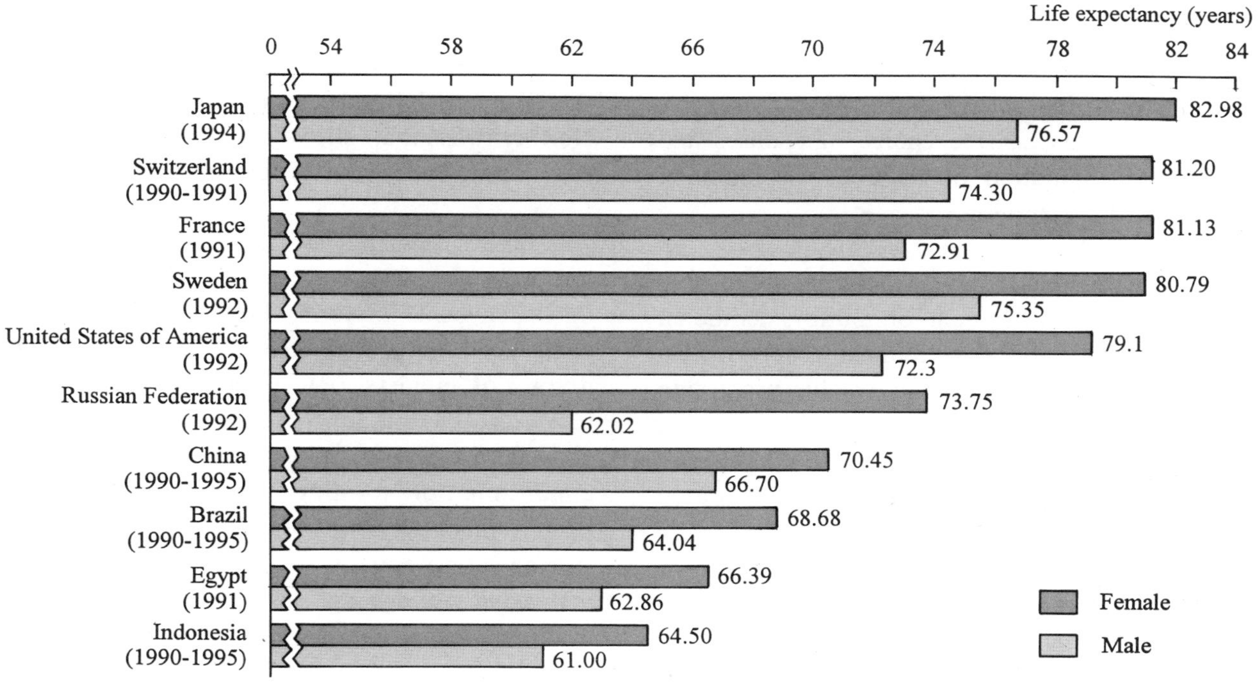

Life expectancy (years)

Country	Female	Male
Japan (1994)	82.98	76.57
Switzerland (1990-1991)	81.20	74.30
France (1991)	81.13	72.91
Sweden (1992)	80.79	75.35
United States of America (1992)	79.1	72.3
Russian Federation (1992)	73.75	62.02
China (1990-1995)	70.45	66.70
Brazil (1990-1995)	68.68	64.04
Egypt (1991)	66.39	62.86
Indonesia (1990-1995)	64.50	61.00

Source: Statistics Bureau, *Statistical Handbook of Japan, 1996* (Tokyo, Government of Japan, 1996).

D. WOMEN IN FAMILY LIFE

1. The Japanese family

In Japan, as in most countries, the family, or *uchi,* has traditionally been the locus of social life. A variety of family forms ranging from the matrilocal customs of the Heian elite to the extreme patrilineality of the *samurai* class in the feudal period had historically existed in the country. Several family forms have also coexisted, especially in the rural areas, and a belief that was common among all family types was the existence of the family/household beyond the life of its current members. During the Tokugawa period, for instance, duty to one's ancestors and respect for one's parents provided the basis for *chonin,* or household continuity, among the upper classes and wealthier merchant and artisan urban households.

However, more rigid family controls than had existed before were institutionalized by the Government with the promulgation of the Domestic Relations and Inheritance Law in 1989. Under this Law, individuals were registered in an official family register, and in the early years of this century, each family was required to conform to the *ie,* or household system. By and large, the *ie* was patterned on the Confucian-influenced multi-generational household of the Tokugawa period upper classes. The head of this household, the oldest male member, had legal authority over and responsibility for all household members. Each generation supplied a male and female adult with a preference for first-son inheritance and patrilocal marriage. Daughters were expected to marry out and younger sons to set up their own households. Women were not entitled to own or control property, nor did they have the freedom to select their spouses. Thus, the *ie* system artificially restricted the development of individualism, individual rights and women's rights.

The years following the end of the Second World War witnessed a radical transformation in Japanese family organization and structure. A new family ideology which gave precedence to individual rights over family obligations was established by the Allied occupation forces. The 1948 revisions to the Civil Code, which closely followed the conjugal family system in the West, removed the predominant legal power of older family heads, and guaranteed equal rights to all female and male family members in regard to inheritance and ownership of property in their own names, free choice of spouses and employment, initiation of divorce and retaining custody of their children.

Although past government policies had favoured the establishment of multi-generational households, available data indicate that extended families constituted a relatively smaller proportion of all households because of the increasing tendency among the non-successor sons (those who were not heirs) to set up their own households. In 1920, for instance, the large majority (55.2 per cent) of all households were nuclear households and only about 38 per cent were extended family households (table 30).

It is also evident from table 30 that the relative share of extended family households in the total number of households has been declining steadily over the years and was reported to be 15.8 per cent in 1995 – less than half the corresponding proportion in 1955. Nevertheless, the fact that about 16 per cent of the Japanese households are still multi-generational clearly indicates that traditional family values and customs continue to be widely prevalent, particularly in regard to providing care for older persons. A recent study also shows that a significant number of older Japanese people still prefer to live with their adult

children, and that the rate of co-residence (or parents and children living together in the same household) in Japan remains high (32 per cent) compared with less than 1 per cent in the United Kingdom of Great Britain and Northern Ireland, slightly over 1 per cent in the United States and 3 per cent in Germany.

The proportion of nuclear family households increased from 55.3 per cent in 1920 to 62.1 per cent in 1965, but since then it has been declining to around 59 per cent. This does not necessarily mean that the trend towards the nuclearization of families has slowed down, but rather that the demographic conditions for forming nuclear families have been temporarily weakened owing to changes in the composition of the population, the increasing average age at marriage, and slowing in internal migration.

However, the remarkable change in household structure that has occurred over the years in Japan is the dramatic increase in single-person households, in both absolute and relative terms. The number of single-person households increased 16-fold, from 664,000 in 1920 to about 10.8 million in 1995, while their proportionate share increased fourfold, from 6.0 to 24.8 per cent, during the same period (table 30; see also figure 10). Indeed, the remarkable increase in the total number of households over the four years has largely been due to the rapid increase in the number of single-person households.

Table 30. Trends in the number of households by family type: selected years, 1920 to 1995

Year	Households by family type										Mean number of house-hold members
	All households		Nuclear family		Extended family		Single member		Non-related		
	(Thou-sands)	(Percent-age)	(Thou-sands)	(Percent-age)	(Thou-sands)	(Percent-age)	(Thou-sands)	(Percent-age)	(Thou-sands)	(Percent-age)	
1920	11 122	100.0	6 152	55.3	4 250	38.2	664	6.0	56	0.5	4.89
1955	17 540	100.0	10 366	59.1	6 353	36.2	596	3.4	225	1.3	4.97
1965	23 280	100.0	14 464	62.1	6 745	29.0	1 795	7.7	276	1.2	4.05
1975	33 596	100.0	19 980	59.5	6 988	20.8	6 561	19.5	67	0.2	3.28
1985	37 980	100.0	22 804	60.0	7 209	19.0	7 895	20.8	72	0.2	3.14
1990	40 670	100.0	24 219	59.6	6 986	17.2	9 390	23.1	75	0.2	2.99
1995	43 447	100.0	25 686	59.1	6 860	15.8	10 768	24.8	133	0.3	2.84

Source: Statistics Bureau, Management and Coordination Agency, *Population Census of Japan* (various years).

Figure 10. Changes in household composition: 1970 to 1994

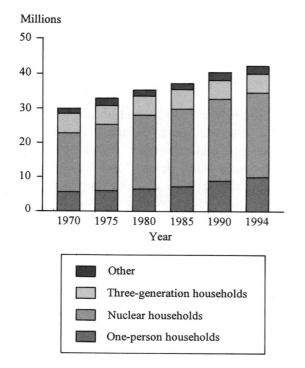

Millions

Other

Three-generation households

Nuclear households

One-person households

Source: Statistics Bureau, *Statistical Handbook of Japan, 1996* (Tokyo, Government of Japan, 1996).

It is also evident from table 30 that the average household size, or mean number of persons per household, has been declining steadily during the four decades, from 4.97 in 1955 to 2.84 in 1995. This remarkable reduction in household size could be attributed to a faster rate of increase in the number of households compared with the rate of population growth, the increasing tendency towards nuclear families and single-member households, and the substantial fall in fertility.

2. Family formation

(a) Marriage patterns

Traditionally, marriage has been a universal phenomenon in Japan because societal norms and values prescribed early marriage for both males and females. Parents have also deemed it their responsibility to have their children married as soon after they reached marriageable age. According to the 1955 census data, nearly 99 per cent of Japanese men and women were ever-married by age 50 years.

According to the 1898 Civil Code, the eligible age for marriage was 18 years for males and 15 years for females. Parental approval was required for the marriage of men under 30 years of age and women under 25 years of age. The new post-war Civil Code, introduced in January 1948, stipulated the minimum age at marriage of 18 years for males and 16 years for females, and parental approval was required for the marriage of males and females under 20 years of age.

Marriage is forbidden only between very close relatives. Though uncles and nieces, or aunts and nephews may not marry, marriage of cousins is permissible. There is also no legal barrier to stop Japanese marrying a foreigner.

Traditionally, there were two types of marriage in Japan. Among peasants and fishermen, particularly in remote rural areas, marriage was often the result of the couple's free choice based on romantic love. There were no sanctions placed on premarital sex between lovers, and the function of the matchmakers in arranging a marriage was purely perfunctory. The only limitation on marriage among the peasantry was the observance and enforcement of village endogamy. On the other hand, marriage among upper-class people, including *samurai* (warriors), landlords and wealthy merchants, was a far more serious matter where consideration of appropriate heritage and status was important. Hence, such marriages were mostly arranged, with the matchmaker playing a very important role. The upper-class spouses rarely knew each other before their marriage and usually met for the first time at the wedding ceremony.

Since the end of the Second World War, marriage based on romantic love has re-emerged in a big way, but even then it has retained aspects of the *samurai* pattern. A number of young people still rely on parents, siblings and close friends to select, investigate and introduce them to potential mates. Such matches are rarely imposed upon the couple, but it is considered most desirable for marriages to arise from arranged meetings.

An interesting feature of the nuptiality pattern in Japan is that, compared with most other Asian countries, the incidence of early marriage, particularly teenage marriage, was very low even in the early part of this century. Despite the fact that the then legal minimum age for marriage was 15 years for females, about 82 per cent of girls aged 15-19 years were reported to be single or never-married at the 1920 census. Even at ages 20-24 years, the proportion of those remaining single has been relatively high, at 31.4 per cent for females and 71.1 per cent for males (table 31).

It is also evident from table 31 that the proportion remaining single or unmarried has been increasing over the years, and that this rising trend has been more pronounced among women than among men. Between 1920 and 1990, the proportion of single or never-married women increased by 17 percentage points at ages 15-19 years, but almost trebled from 31.4 to 86.0 per cent at ages 20-24 years, and increased more than fourfold from 9.2 to 40.4 per cent at ages 25-29 years. Data from the censuses also indicate that even at ages beyond 30 years, there were very substantial increases in the proportion of single women during this 70-year period.

The proportion of never-married or single men at various ages also increased between 1920 and 1990, but the pace of this increase was slower than that for women at ages 15-30 years because the corresponding proportion for men was already high in 1920 and considerably higher than that for females at each age group. Even in 1990, a higher proportion of males compared with females remained single or unmarried at all ages (table 31).

Despite the rising trend in the proportion remaining single, most Japanese people marry at least once and, according to the 1990 census data, the proportion opting for celibacy was 6.8 per cent among men and 4.6 per cent among women aged 45-49 years. Nevertheless, the fact that about 7 per cent of men and 5 per cent of women aged 45-49 years were reported to be never-married in 1990 means that marriage is no longer universal in Japan.

The continuous increase in the proportion single at various ages is also reflected in a rise in the average age at first marriage. Available data indicate that the average age at first marriage was already rising in Japan in the pre-war period but declined temporarily during the period of the first marriage boom in the post-war period. As will be noted from table 32, the average age at first marriage has generally been rising since 1950, and was 28.5 years for men and 26.2 years for women in 1994. The rise in the average age at marriage

Table 31. Percentage of single persons by age group and sex: 1920 to 1990

Sex/age group	1920	1930	1940	1950	1960	1970	1980	1990
Male								
15-19	97.3	99.0	99.6	99.5	99.8	99.3	99.7	99.7
20-24	71.1	79.7	90.9	82.9	91.6	90.0	91.8	93.6
25-29	25.8	28.8	42.0	34.5	46.1	46.5	55.2	65.4
30-34	8.1	8.1	10.3	8.0	9.9	11.7	21.5	32.8
35-39	4.1	3.9	4.4	3.2	3.6	45.7	8.5	19.1
40-44	2.8	2.4	2.7	1.9	2.0	2.8	4.7	11.8
45-49	2.3	1.8	2.0	1.5	1.4	1.9	3.1	6.8
Female								
15-19	82.3	89.3	95.7	96.6	98.6	97.8	99.0	99.3
20-24	31.4	37.7	53.5	55.3	68.3	71.6	77.8	86.0
25-29	9.2	8.4	13.5	15.2	21.6	18.1	24.0	40.4
30-34	4.1	3.7	5.2	5.7	9.4	7.2	9.1	13.9
35-39	2.7	2.4	2.9	3.0	5.5	5.8	5.5	7.5
40-44	1.9	1.8	2.0	2.0	3.2	5.3	4.4	7.4
45-49	1.7	1.6	1.6	1.5	2.1	4.0	4.4	4.6

Source: Statistics Bureau, Management and Coordination Agency, *Population Census of Japan* (various years).

as well as of the proportions remaining single, particularly at the popular marriage ages means that women are delaying their marriage for a variety of reasons. As noted earlier, the average level of educational attainment is rising, more women are working, and there is a feeling that young women workers have increasingly strong career aspirations. In addition, the economic burdens of marriage and rearing a family are widely recognized, and the accumulation of financial resources prior to marriage is often necessary just to be able to afford suitable housing. Changing social attitudes about the institution of marriage, and some reluctance on the part of men to accept such changes, are also important contributing factors.

Table 32. Average age at first marriage: selected years, 1920 to 1994

| Year | Mean age at first marriage | | |
	Groom	Bride	Difference
1920	27.4	23.2	4.2
1930	27.3	23.2	4.1
1940	29.0	24.6	4.4
1943	29.5	25.0	4.5
1947	26.1	22.9	3.2
1950	25.9	23.0	2.9
1955	26.6	23.8	2.8
1960	27.2	24.4	2.8
1965	27.2	24.5	2.7
1970	26.9	24.2	2.7
1975	27.0	24.7	2.3
1980	27.8	25.2	2.6
1985	28.2	25.5	2.7
1990	28.4	25.9	2.5
1994	28.5	26.2	2.3

Source: Ministry of Health and Welfare.

(b) Reproductive behaviour

Apart from shifts in marriage practices and patterns, there have also been radical changes in the reproductive behaviour of Japanese women over the past 75 years. In particular, the attitudes of married couples towards desired family size have undergone significant transformation, as evidenced by the dramatic decline in the number of children parents produce and the increasing prevalence of contraceptive practice among Japanese couples.

The total fertility rate (TFR), or the number of children that would be born to a woman during her reproductive period if she survived throughout that period and experienced the same age-specific fertility rates as those prevailing during the period of reference, for selected years from 1920 to 1923, is shown in table 33.

Table 33. Total fertility rate: selected years, 1920 to 1993

Year	Total fertility rate
1920	5.24
1930	4.71
1940	4.11
1947	4.54
1950	3.65
1955	2.37
1960	2.00
1965	2.14
1971	2.16
1973	2.14
1975	1.91
1980	1.85
1985	1.76
1990	1.50
1993	1.46

Source: Ministry of Health and Welfare.

It will be noted from table 33 that in 1920, a Japanese woman had, on the average, 5.24 children during her entire reproductive period. But since then, TFR declined slowly to reach 4.54 in 1947, and thereafter rapidly, by more than half, to 2.00 children per woman, or below replacement level, in 1960. Although there were only minor fluctuations around the replacement level until 1973, subsequently TFR started to fall again, to 1.46 in 1993. In other words, today a Japanese woman has, on the average, 3.25 children fewer than her counterpart in 1947 and 3.78 fewer than her counterpart in 1920.

The decline in TFR has been attributed to two important factors: an increase in female age at marriage, or postponement of marriage, by young women; and the decline in marital fertility or fertility.

As noted earlier, the average age at first marriage for females rose from 23.0 years in

1950 to 26.2 years in 1994 (table 32). The postponement of marriage by young women is due to a variety of reasons, including longer average educational tenure and longer duration of employment. Several studies have shown that there is a strong positive correlation between marriage duration and fertility, which is attributed to the length of exposure to the risk of pregnancy. The commonly held hypothesis is that late marriage has a dampening effect on fertility. A 1995 study also concluded that, since the early 1970s, the delay of marriage has been playing a principal role in the Japanese fertility decline.

Available evidence indicates that an important factor that had contributed to the fertility decline in Japan has been the desire on the part of parents to limit their family size, and this desire had existed from the early part of this century. Japan experienced economic prosperity during the First World War, but the depression that followed the war (1919-1925) caused considerable hardships to the people, especially the working class. Consequently, social movements for the betterment of workers' living conditions advocated the need for birth control as a measure to ensure the health and welfare of the people, as well as for the emancipation of women.

Since knowledge about family planning was limited and the contraceptives then available not sufficiently reliable, induced abortion, which was illegal and severely restricted, was resorted to in order to terminate unwanted pregnancies. In 1948, the Government enacted the Eugenics Protection Law liberalizing the grounds for abortion, and consequently there was a rapid rise in the incidence of induced abortion to about one million in 1950, raising concerns about the effects of this practice on the health of women. In 1951, family planning was adopted as a government policy, and in 1952, the Ministry of Health and Welfare launched the national family planning programme to promote knowledge about and use of contraceptives through specially trained family planning field workers, such as midwives and public health nurses.

As a result of the various measures adopted, there have been remarkable increases in the proportion of women using contraceptive methods. Data available from various surveys indicate that the prevalence rate increased from about 20 per cent in 1950 to 60 per cent in 1970 and that the pace of this increase was most rapid in the early part of this 20-year period. Since 1980, the level of use has fluctuated between 60 and 65 per cent (figure 11), which is somewhat below the level reached in most other developed countries.

Figure 11. Trends in contraceptive use by method in Japan: 1950 to 1990

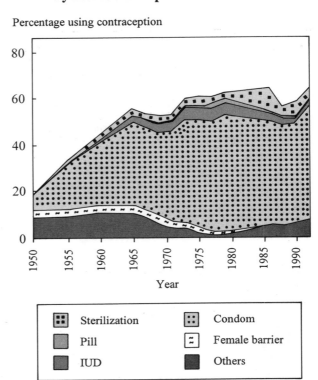

Source: United Nations, *Levels and Trends of Contraceptive Use as Assessed in 1994* (New York, 1996).

The relatively low contraceptive **prevalence** rate in Japan compared with many other developed countries could be due to two factors. First, it is possible that the use of non-supply or traditional methods has been under-reported in Japanese surveys owing to the manner in which the questions were posed. The second factor is the inclusion of women aged 45-49 years in the Japanese surveys and their exclusion from samples in most other developed countries. Perhaps owing to the onset of menopause, contraceptive prevalence is considerably lower among women aged 45-49 years compared with those aged 30-40 years. According to the 1992 Japanese survey, the contraceptive prevalence rate was 67 per cent for ages under 45 years but 64 per cent for ages under 50 years.

There are three important aspects to be noted in regard to the widespread adoption of family planning practice in Japan in recent decades. First, the practice was adopted on a voluntary basis and the demand for family planning services originated from the people themselves. As noted earlier, the need to limit the number of births has been recognized by Japanese parents since the early part of this century, and the widespread practice of this limitation after the Second World War was no sudden or new phenomenon but may well be regarded as the resurgence of a traditional behaviour pattern. It is true that there were a series of discussions in the mass media regarding birth control, but these discussions were not organized for the purpose of motivating the people to practise contraception but rather to meet their felt needs to obtain more knowledge about the subject. Further, the planning of family size is generally considered to be typical behaviour that accompanies the modernization process. In the case of Japan, the concept of family size was first adopted by the people in the face of difficult economic conditions but later, with increasing industrialization and modernization, became an accepted norm. The Government's programmes for the promotion of family planning were not intended to induce the desire for a small family, but were primarily launched to assist parents in achieving their desired family size.

Second, although the government programmes did play a significant role in reducing the population growth rate, they were operated for the purpose of protecting the health of women and family welfare. Reflecting this concept, in 1959, the mandate for administering family planning activities was transferred within the Ministry of Health and Welfare from the Public Health's Bureau to the Children's Bureau (now the Children and Families Bureau), and implemented in relation to maternal and child health activities.

Third, in addition to the Government, a number of private voluntary associations have involved themselves in promoting family planning activities in Japan. In particular, these voluntary organizations have carried out a series of family planning programmes among workers in large organized enterprises. Under the title of "New life movement", family planning was presented as an integral part of the campaign for a better life.

It is also interesting to note that, while in almost all other Asian countries the most popular modern methods of contraception are those used by women, in Japan the methods used by males (condoms and male sterilization), constitute about 85 per cent of the modern methods in use, with condoms alone accounting for 80 per cent of these methods (figure 11). Since 1975, more than three quarters of the couples have relied on condoms as their main family planning method, and Japan has the highest condom use rate among the industrialized countries of the world. Coitus interuptus had been the second leading method of birth control, but the rate declined from a high of 46.1 per cent in 1959 to 16.3 per cent in 1988.

Several reasons have been advanced for the very high condom acceptance rate in Japan. First, the method is inexpensive, easy to use, requires no elaborate preparation or special instructions, and needs no individual examination or fitting. Second, it has been pointed out that Japanese couples prefer condoms to methods that require surgery, the insertion of foreign objects, or the use of chemicals, despite the advantages that these methods offer. Third, although Japan has been traditionally a male-dominant society, males participate widely in family planning since they seem as highly motivated as their wives, with the wives being dependent on husbands to make the decision and take the initiative. It is only with the understanding and cooperation of males that condoms could have become the most widely used method. Fourth, the condoms manufactured in

Japan are "better products in a better package with better promotion", owing mainly to their thinness and lightness. Besides, condoms are made available through a wide variety of outlets, inlcuding drug stores, vending machines, super-markets, mail order, visiting saleswomen, and local distribution systems run by women's organizations.

The increasing use of contraceptive methods has resulted in a reduction in the incidence of induced abortions. Available data indicate that the number of reported cases of abortion declined from a peak of 1.17 million (68 per 100 births) in 1955 to 460,000 (38 per 100 births) in 1990. Despite this decline, Japan has one of the highest abortion rates among the world's industrialized countries. According to a 1987 survey, 10.7 per cent of pregnancies were terminated through induced abortion, but this figure probably understates the actual incidence level. The abortion rate rises dramatically after the second birth, this method being used to terminate 18.3 per cent of the third pregnancy, 36.7 per cent of the fourth, and 45.6 per cent of the fifth. Available information also suggests that the incidence of abortion among teenage girls has been increasing in recent years. The high overall abortion rate reflects the liberaliza-tion of the legal grounds for abortion, as well as the fact that the two most popular methods, condoms and coitus interruptus, are not always reliable.

3. Marital disruption

Disruption in married life occurs as a result of widowhood or of divorce/separation. These events seriously affect family life. They also have important demographic implications by reducing the number of currently married persons and, depending on the ages at which they occur, the number of births.

The age-sex-specific proportions of wid-owed and divorced persons (calculated as the percentage of ever-married persons) from the data of the 1980 and 1990 population censuses are shown in table 34.

It will be noted from table 34 that the overall proportions widowed and divorced have been significantly higher for females than for males. In 1990, for instance, the proportion of ever-married females aged 15 years and over who were reported to be widowed was 16.7 per cent, or nearly five times the corresponding

Table 34. Percentage widowed and divorced among ever-married persons aged 15 years and over by age group and sex: 1980 and 1990

Age group	Percentage widowed				Percentage divorced			
	1980		1990		1980		1990	
	Male	Female	Male	Female	Male	Female	Male	Female
15-19	0.1	0.1	0.1	0.2	0.9	1.0	1.1	1.8
20-24	0.2	0.1	0.2	0.2	1.2	1.4	2.0	2.9
25-29	0.1	0.2	0.1	0.2	1.2	1.8	1.9	2.7
30-34	0.1	0.5	0.1	0.4	1.5	2.6	2.1	3.3
35-39	0.3	1.3	0.3	0.8	1.8	3.2	2.8	4.6
40-44	0.5	2.8	0.5	2.2	2.0	3.5	3.5	7.3
45-49	0.9	5.2	0.9	3.5	2.1	3.8	3.7	5.6
50-54	1.7	9.4	1.5	6.8	1.9	4.3	3.5	5.0
55-59	2.4	17.8	2.5	11.6	1.8	4.3	2.9	4.5
60-64	4.7	29.9	4.1	19.0	1.6	3.4	2.2	4.4
65-69	8.1	44.6	6.4	32.3	1.5	2.8	1.8	4.1
70-74	14.2	64.1	9.9	50.2	1.3	2.5	1.5	3.2
75-79	23.7	73.6	16.2	66.9	1.2	1.9	1.3	2.5
80-84	36.2	85.3	26.7	81.1	1.1	1.7	1.1	2.0
85+	54.1	93.3	45.9	92.0	1.1	1.7	1.0	1.7
All ages 15+	3.4	15.8	3.5	16.7	1.7	3.1	2.7	4.4

Source: Statistics Bureau, Management and Coordination Agency, *Population Census of Japan,* 1980 and 1990.

proportion of 3.5 per cent reported for males. In that year, the overall proportion of the divorced among females, 4.4 per cent, was more than one and a half times the 2.7 per cent reported among males. Similar gender disparities were disclosed by the 1980 census.

The incidence of widowhood is a function of mortality, and since the risks of death increase with advancing age, the incidence of widowhood also increases with age. Further, since mortality rates at all ages are higher for Japanese males compared with their female counterparts, the incidence of widowhood is also higher among females than among males at all ages. This gender disparity, in terms of percentage points, is more pronounced at older than at younger ages. In 1990, the proportion widowed among females exceeded that among males by more than 50 percentage points at ages 75 to 84 years; and at ages 85 years and over, 92 per cent of females as against about 4.6 per cent of males were reported to be widowed.

It is also evident from table 34 that the overall proportions divorced among the ever-married are considerably lower than the proportions widowed. However, there has been an increase in the proportions divorced from 1.7 to 2.7 per cent for males and from 3.1 to 4.4 per cent for females, and these increases have occurred at all age groups.

Data from other sources (not included in table 34) also indicate that while the number of marriages dropped by 30.5 per cent between 1970 and 1988, the number of divorces increased by 58.4 per cent during the same period. Consequently, the number of registered divorces as a proportion of the number of registered marriages had increased from 9.3 per cent in 1970 to 58.4 per cent in 1988. In absolute terms, the number of reported divorces increased from about 96,000 in 1970 to 155,600 in 1988, and further to reach a record high of 195,000 in 1994.

It will also be noted from table 34 that the proportion of ever-married reported as being divorced is higher among females than among males at all ages, and that the proportions for both males and females are considerably higher at ages 35-59 years than at the younger and older ages. Available studies also indicate that while in 1970 the chief cause of disruption of marriage of at least 11 years' duration was the death of a partner, since 1975 divorce has become the chief cause for the dissolution of long-term marriages. The proportion of disrupted marriages of 11-12 years' duration due to divorce increased from 47.8 per cent in 1970 to 59.5 per cent in 1975, and further to 74.4 per cent in 1988.

All available evidence clearly indicates that in recent decades the incidence of divorce has risen sharply in Japan, a phenomenon attributed to a variety of factors. In the past, bad or non-compatible marriages were endured because women had no alternative but to depend on their husbands for economic support. But with the increasing employment of women in salaried jobs, they have become self-supporting. Further, social mores have been changing over the years and Japanese people have become much more accepting of divorce in recent years. The incidence of divorce among older couples has also been increasing, owing largely to the husband's retirement. The "company first" mentality of salaried men in Japan has already led to some estrangement among couples, and the retirement of the husband generates new pressures and burdens that undermine the already weak relationships between husband and wife.

It must also be emphasized that the official data understate considerably the reality of broken marriages in Japan where there is no concept of divorce within marriage, regardless of whether the couple is formally separated or not. There is strong pressure to maintain appearances for the sake of the children, career, family name etc., and for many wives there is still no viable economic alternative. Many lack the skills to re-enter the labour market. In addition, child support and alimony payments are not strictly enforced by law.

4. Fatherless families

Accordingly to surveys carried out by the Ministry of Health and Welfare, the number of fatherless families in Japan increased by 34 per cent from 633,700 in 1978 to 849,200 in 1988. This increase was largely the result of a rise in the number of divorces in the country. Data from the surveys also show that the proportion of fatherless families resulting from the divorce of parents increased from 37.9 to 62.3 per cent between 1978 and 1988. Consequently, there has been a decline in the proportions of fatherless families resulting from the father's death, unwed mothers, and other causes such as desertion or abandonment by the father (table 35).

The average age of the mothers in fatherless families has been declining over the years owing to an increase in the relative share of the mothers aged less than 40 years, from 35.3 per cent in 1978 to 42.2 per cent in 1988 (table 36).

In divorced households, the children usually stay with the mother, and sometimes the child-support payment provided by the father is inadequate to meet the various requirements of the children. In practically all fatherless families, the mother is both the primary income-earner and the person responsible for raising the children. Since these families often face economic, social and psychological insecurity, various schemes have been devised to guarantee income and secure adequate living conditions for them.

The various measures adopted to assist fatherless families include the payment of survivors' pensions to those families in which the father has died; and payment of allowances for child-rearing to those families that are fatherless as a result of the divorce of the parents. Further, there are 13 loan schemes designed to help the mothers support their families. The loans may be used to cover expenses for starting a business, education of the children and housing. Other measures to promote self-reliance include the dispatch of care-takers, the provision of counselling services, the opening of job opportunities and the promotion of employment, giving favourable

Table 35. Number of fatherless families and their percentage distribution according to the cause of incidence: 1978, 1983 and 1988

Year	Number of fatherless families	Percentage distribution by cause of incidence				
		Father's death	Parents' divorce	Unwed mother	Other	Total
1978	633 700	49.9	37.9	4.8	7.4	100.0
1983	718 100	36.1	49.1	5.3	9.5	100.0
1988	849 200	29.7	62.3	3.6	4.4	100.0

Source: Ministry of Health and Welfare, *National Survey of Fatherless Families* (various years).

Table 36. Percentage distribution of mothers in fatherless families by broad age groups: 1978, 1983 and 1988

Year	Percentage of mothers at ages					
	Below 30 years	30-39 years	40-49 years	50-59 years	60 years and over	All ages
1978	5.6	29.7	49.5	13.4	1.9	100.0
1983	5.4	33.5	46.9	12.3	1.9	100.0
1988	6.5	35.7	46.4	11.1	0.3	100.0

Source: Ministry of Health and Welfare, *National Survey of Fatherless Families* (various years).

consideration for placement in public housing, and management of homes for fatherless families. Some tax exemptions and deductions are also specially available to those families.

E. WOMEN IN ECONOMIC LIFE

1. Labour-force participation

Although females constitute more than half of the population of Japan in the working ages 15 years and over, they account for a considerably lower proportion of the labour force at those ages. In 1980, females formed 51.4 per cent of all Japanese aged 15 years and over but only 38.7 per cent of the national labour force. Between 1980 and 1995, the total labour force increased by 18 per cent, from 56.5 million to 66.7 million, but this increase was more pronounced in the case of the female than the male labour force. Whereas the male labour force increased by 14.5 per cent from 34.7 million to 39.7 million, the female labour force increased by 22 per cent, from about 21.9 million to 27.0 million, during the same 15-year period. Consequently, the relative share of females in the total labour force had risen to 40.5 per cent by 1995 (annex table E.1). This increase is also reflected in a rise in the female overall labour-force participation rate (female labour force as a percentage of the female population aged 15 years and over) from 47.6 per cent in 1980 to 50.0 per cent in 1995 (table 37).

It will also be noted from table 37 that the overall participation rate has always been higher for males than for females but that this gender gap has generally been narrowing since 1975 owing to the increasing participation of females in the labour force. Several factors, such as the economic recovery after the 1974-1975 recession and stable growth rates; the increased demand for female workers by the expanding service industry; the economic pressure of sluggish growth in family incomes; and women's desire to work, have contributed to the increasing participation of women in the labour force.

The age-specific labour-force participation rates for males and females have also been significantly different in two respects. First, the male rates continue to be higher than the female rates at all ages excepting the 20-26 age group, in which the female rate was almost equal to or higher than the male rate in most of the years, although the female rates at ages 25-54 years have generally been increasing since 1980 (annex table E.2).

Second, the male participation rate rises sharply with age until ages 25-29 years, and then rises slowly to reach a peak around 98 per cent at ages 35-39 years, thereafter declining gradually until ages 55-59 years and then more rapidly to around 40 per cent at ages 65 years and over. The female participation rate, on the other hand, rises sharply to reach a peak at ages 20-24 years, thereafter declining gradually up to ages 30-34 years and then rising to reach a second peak at ages 45-49, declining thereafter. In other words, while the male age-specific labour-force participation

Table 37. Trends in overall labour-force participation rates by sex: 1965 to 1995

Year	Labour-force participation rate (percentage)			
	Both sexes	Male	Female	Male/female difference
1965	65.7	81.7	50.6	31.1
1970	65.4	81.8	49.9	31.9
1975	63.0	81.4	45.7	35.7
1980	63.3	79.8	47.6	32.2
1985	63.0	78.1	48.7	29.4
1990	63.3	77.2	50.1	27.1
1995	63.4	77.6	50.0	27.6

Source: Statistics Bureau, Management and Coordination Agency, *Labour Force Survey* (various years).

rates assume the shape of an inverted U, the female rates form an M-shaped curve, with two peaks at ages 20-24 and 45-49 years and a sharp drop at ages 30-34 years (see figure 12).

Marriage and childbearing and child-rearing appear to have a major influence on women's labour-force participation in Japan. During the period when they remain single, most women participate in the labour force, and consequently the female labour-force participation rate is highest during these years. Some women retire from work when they marry or have children. Most women who previously withdrew from work re-enter the labour market when their children reach schooling age.

In recent years, however, the trough between the two peaks in the age pattern of female labour-force participation has become shallow, with an increase in labour-force participation rates from 43.9 in 1975 to 53.3 in 1995 at ages 30-34 years and from 54.0 to 59.3 per cent at ages 35-39 during the same period. This reflects the recent trend in female labour-force participation and signifies the emergence of a group of women who remain single and

continue working, as well as an increase in the participation rate of those who do not stop working when they marry or of those who have children but continue working.

It is also clear from annex table E.2 that there has been a dramatic decline in labour-force participation rates at ages 15-19 years for both males and females. The male participation rate almost halved, from 36.3 per cent in 1976 to 18.8 per cent in 1995, while the female rate more than halved, from 35.8 to 15.6 per cent, during the 30-year period. These declines at the youngest age group reflect the rising participation of boys and girls in the education system.

2. Employed labour force

The labour force includes both employed and unemployed persons over a stipulated age. In terms of the definitions adopted in the Japanese censuses and labour-force surveys, employed persons are those who performed any work during the week prior to the date of the census/survey for pay or profit such as wage, salary, allowance, business profit etc. Those

Figure 12. Age-specific labour-force participation rates by sex: 1960 and 1995

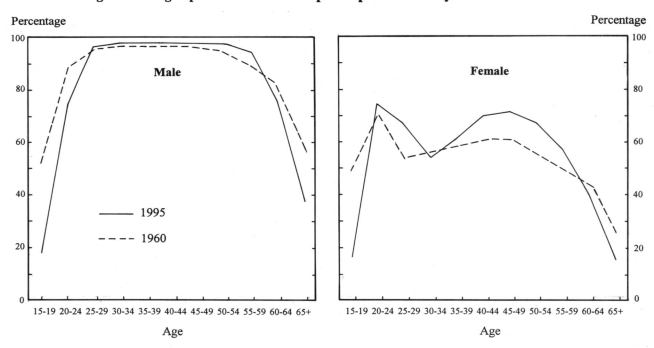

Source: Statistics Bureau Management and Coordination Agency, *Statistical Handbook of Japan, 1996* (Tokyo, Government of Japan, 1996).

who had a job or business but did not work at all during the reference week because of vacation, illness, bad weather, labour disputes or for personal reasons are also regarded as employed provided that (a) in the case of employees, their absence from work did not extend over 30 days up to the date of the census/survey, or they received or expected to receive wage or salary during the reference week; and (b) in the case of self-employed workers, their absence from work did not exceed 30 days up to the date of the census/survey. Persons working for a family enterprise such as on a farm, in a store, or in a private hospital etc., though not paid any wages, are also considered as being employed.

(a) Employment rate

Data from the labour-force surveys indicate that the employment rate, or the employed as a proportion of the labour force, ranged between 97 and 98 per cent for both males and females between 1980 and 1995 (table 38).

Table 38. Employment rate by sex: 1980 to 1995

| Year | Employment rate | | |
	Both sexes	Male	Female
1980	98.0	98.0	98.0
1985	97.4	97.4	97.3
1990	97.9	97.9	97.8
1995	96.9	96.9	96.8

Source: Annex table E.1.

It is also evident from annex table E.1 that the total number of employed persons had increased by 9.2 million, from 55.4 million in 1980 to 64.6 million in 1995, representing an increase by 16.6 per cent over the 15-year period. But this increase was more pronounced in respect of employed females than employed males. Whereas the number of employed males increased by 4.49 million, or 13.2 per cent, the number of employed females increased by 4.72 million, or 22.0 per cent, during the same period. In other words, women accounted for

more than half the increase in the number of employed persons between 1980 and 1995.

(b) Employment characteristics

The nature of the economic activity in which an employed person is engaged could be viewed from three perspectives: (a) the industry or the activity of the establishment in which the employed person works during the time reference period; (b) the occupation or kind of work performed during the time reference period; and (c) the employment status as either employer, paid employee, self-employed, family worker etc.

The proportionate distribution of the employed persons by major industrial group in 1995 is given in table 39.

It will be noted from table 39 that nearly 62 per cent of the employed labour force was engaged in the tertiary-sector industries (utilities, transport and communications, trade, finance and insurance, services and government) and that this proportion was substantially higher for females (69.5 per cent) than for males (56.7 per cent). Within the tertiary sector, the service industry is the single largest employer, with 31.6 per cent of employed females and 20.3 per cent of employed males, followed by the wholesale and retail trade, absorbing 28.1 per cent of employed females and 19.3 per cent of employed males. A considerably higher proportion of employed males (8.4 per cent) than employed females (2.5 per cent) work in the transport and communication industry.

The secondary sector (comprising mining, construction and manufacturing) is the second most important source of employment, with 37.2 per cent of employed males and 23.2 per cent of employed females; within this broad group, the manufacturing industry is the leading employer, absorbing 22.5 per cent of the employed males and 19.1 per cent of the total employed females. The proportion of employed males working in the construction industry is more than three times the corresponding proportion for females. A higher

Table 39. Percentage distribution of employed persons by major industrial group and sex: 1995

Major industrial group	Both sexes	Male	Female
Primary industry	**5.96**	**5.56**	**6.54**
Agriculture, forestry and fisheries	5.96	5.56	6.54
Secondary industry	**31.57**	**37.15**	**23.17**
Mining	0.09	0.13	0.04
Construction	10.34	14.50	4.07
Manufacturing	21.13	22.52	19.06
Tertiary industry	**61.80**	**56.67**	**69.53**
Electricity, gas, heat supply and water	0.57	0.80	0.21
Transport and communications	6.06	8.42	2.52
Wholesale and retail trade, eating and drinking establishments	22.79	19.28	28.07
Finance, insurance and real estate	4.18	3.56	5.12
Services	24.84	20.34	31.61
Government	3.36	4.27	1.99
Establishment not adequately described	**0.67**	**0.61**	**0.76**
Total	**100.00**	**100.00**	**100.00**

Source: Statistics Bureau, Management and Coordination Agency, *1995 Population Census of Japan,* vol. 3-1, *Labour Force Status of Population, Industry (Major Groups) of Employed Persons* (Tokyo, Government of Japan, 1997).

proportion among employed females (6.5 per cent) compared with employed males (5.6 per cent) is engaged in primary-sector industries, which include agriculture, forestry and fisheries.

The pattern of occupational distribution also varies somewhat between females and males. While the largest proportion of employed females (29.5 per cent) were engaged as clerical and related workers, the largest concentration of employed males and the second largest concentration of employed females were in the major occupational category of craftsmen, mining, production process and construction workers and labourers. The proportion employed as sales workers was higher for males (15.5 per cent) compared with females (13.8 per cent) but the proportion employed as service workers among females (12.5 per cent) was nearly twice that among males (4.7 per cent). A slightly higher proportion among females (13.3 per cent) than among males (11.9 per cent) were working as professional and technical workers in 1995 (table 40).

In most countries, employed persons are classified into four employment status categories: employees, employers, self-employed, and unpaid family workers. But in view of the special employment conditions specific to the country, all employed persons in Japan are classified into the following six employment status categories:

(1) *Employees,* or those employed by a person, a company, a corporation or a government office etc., including office workers, factory workers, public servants, officers of a corporation, employees in a private retail shop, domestic servants, daily or temporary workers etc.

(2) *Directors* of a company or a corporation, including managing directors

(3) *Self-employed employing others,* or persons who run a business employing others, that is, proprietors of private shops and factories, farmers, medical practitioners, lawyers, who have one or more employees

(4) *Self-employed not employing others,* or persons who run a business without employees

(5) *Family workers,* or persons who work in a business, farm, trade, or professional enterprise operated by a member of the household in which they live

(6) *Persons doing home handicrafts,* or persons engaged in handicraft work within the household

Table 40. Percentage distribution of employed persons by major occupational category and sex: 1995

Major occupational category	Both sexes	Male	Female
Professional and related workers	12.48	11.94	13.30
Managers and officials	4.14	6.21	1.02
Clerical and related workers	18.90	11.82	29.54
Sales workers	14.82	15.48	13.82
Service workers	7.84	4.74	12.50
Protective service workers	1.46	2.32	0.17
Agricultural, forestry and fisheries workers	5.94	5.61	6.42
Workers in transport and communication occupations	3.72	5.87	0.49
Craftsmen, mining, production process and construction workers and labourers	30.10	35.45	22.06
Workers not classified by occupations	0.60	0.56	0.68
All occupations	100.00	100.00	100.00

Source: Statistics Bureau, Management and Coordination Agency, *1995 Population Census of Japan,* vol. 4-1, *Occupation (Major Groups) of Employed Persons, Types of Households* (Tokyo, Government of Japan, 1997).

The percentage distribution of employed persons according to the above six employment status categories and sex in 1995 is shown in table 41.

It will be noted from table 41 that the vast majority (75.3 per cent) of all employed persons were engaged as paid employees in 1995, but that this proportion was slightly higher among females (76.1 per cent) than among males (74.8 per cent). Further, while the second largest proportion of employed males are in self-employment (15.6 per cent), family work is the second most important "employment sector" for women, with 13.5 per cent of employed females being reported as family workers in the 1995 census. A sizeable proportion of employed women (5.89 per cent) were also reported to be in self-employment at the 1995 census.

Available evidence also shows that between 1975 and 1995, the total number of employees increased by 32.4 per cent, from 36.46 million to 48.29 million. But the number of female employees increased from 11.67 million to 19.49 million, or by 67 per cent, far exceeding the growth rate of the total number of employees.

The rapid increase in female employees has also been accompanied by significant changes in the pattern of their industrial attachment. In 1975, the largest proportion of the female employees worked in the manufacturing sector (30.96 per cent), followed by the service sector (26.76 per cent) and the wholesale and

Table 41. Percentage distribution of employed persons by employment status and sex: 1995

Employment status	Both sexes	Male	Female
Employees	75.29	74.76	76.09
Directors	5.90	7.59	3.37
Self-employed, employing others	3.36	4.59	1.51
Self-employed, not employing others	8.34	10.96	4.38
Family workers	6.62	2.04	13.50
Persons doing home handicrafts	0.49	0.05	1.15
Total	100.00	100.00	100.00

Source: Statistics Bureau, Management and Coordination Agency, *1995 Population Census of Japan,* vol. 3-1, *Labour Force Status of Population, Industry (Major Groups) of Employed Persons* (Tokyo, Government of Japan, 1997).

retail trade sector (24.87 per cent). Since then the relative share of female employees has been increasing in the service and trade sectors and decreasing in the manufacturing sector; by 1995, the service and trade sectors had surpassed the manufacturing sector as the largest and second-largest employers of females respectively. However, the combined share of all these three sectors in the total female employees increased slightly, from 82.59 per cent in 1975 to 83.16 per cent in 1995. It is thus clear that most of the increases in the number of female employees occurred in tertiary-sector industries, particularly the service and trade sectors. The relative share of female employees in the primary sector registered a slight decrease between 1975 and 1995 (table 42).

Another important aspect of the rise in female employment is the increase in female part-time employment. In Japan, practically all industrial and commercial establishments resort to the practice of hiring workers on a part-time basis so as to offset the rigidities of the country's employment system. Part-time workers often work nearly full-time hours but are accorded the same level of wages, benefits or job security as that enjoyed by full-time core employees, who are mostly male. Thus, part-time workers serve as "shock-absorbers", enabling the establishment to adjust to business cycle fluctuations.

Data from labour-force surveys and other sources show that part-time work was already on the rise before the oil crisis, but has been growing even more in recent years. According to available information, the relative share among total female employees of those working 35 hours or less per week increased rapidly, from 12.2 per cent in 1970 to 19.3 in 1980, and further to 27.9 per cent in 1990 and 31.2 per cent in 1993. Thus, today about one third of all female employees are engaged on a part-time basis in Japan.

The reported rising trends in female part-time employment are also a manifestation of the "background" to the participation of women in social labour, and are clearly linked to the gender division of responsibilities within the family, the economic conditions of households, and the acceptability and aptness of part-time work to particular categories of women. In most urban families, where the husbands commute to work and return late, having little time to spend with children or help with domestic chores, the wife assumes full responsibility for raising the children, running the household and managing the family budget. A 1994 National Survey of the Contemporary Family conducted by the Nibon University, for instance, revealed that over 60 per cent of the male respondents did not devote any time at all to housework, child care, cooking, and

Table 42. Percentage distribution of female employees by major industrial sector:
1975, 1985 and 1995

Major industrial sector	1975	1985	1995
Agriculture, forestry and fisheries	0.77	0.78	0.64
Mining	0.09	0.06	0.04
Construction	4.20	3.68	3.43
Manufacturing	30.96	28.10	20.84
Transportation, communications and public utilities	3.60	2.98	3.32
Wholesale and retail trade and eating and drinking establishments	24.87	26.36	27.09
Finance, insurance and real estate	6.09	5.81	5.91
Services	26.76	29.97	35.23
Government service	2.66	2.26	2.62
Establishment not adequately described	–	–	0.88
Total	100.00	100.00	100.00

Source: Statistics Bureau, Management and Coordination Agency, *Labour Force Survey,* 1975 and 1985; and *Population Census,* 1995.

cleaning up after meals. In such situations, the wives can, if necessary, take up only part-time work outside the home.

Available evidence also indicates that for most families, the earnings of the husbands alone are not adequate to meet household expenses, including loan repayments and the costs of children's education. Hence, it had become necessary for the wives to work also, in order to augment the family income. However, given their full-time responsibility for household management, the wives can only work on a part-time basis. According to the Family Income and Expenditure Survey conducted by the Statistics Bureau, Management and Coordination Agency, the earnings of the wife and income from other sources account, on the average, for about 12 per cent of the actual household income.

Further, a larger number of women than men are striving to seek higher levels of education and training in order to acquire work skills appropriate for high-pay employment. The desire for "self-realization" is particularly strong among rural women who had migrated to cities in pursuit of better employment opportunities. For such women, part-time employment offers the opportunity to earn income to support themselves while at the same time pursuing their studies.

As noted earlier, about 13.5 per cent of all employed females are engaged as family workers, and family work constitutes the second most important avenue of employment for females (table 41). According to data from the 1995 population census, about 36 per cent of all female family workers were employed in the agriculture and allied sector, and a further about 29 per cent in the trade sector, 13.7 per cent in the service sector and 10.4 per cent in the manufacturing sector (table 43).

Within the agricultural sector, female family workers constituted about 74 per cent of all employed females. Most women engaged in agriculture have not received basic training in agricultural techniques and management. This not only results in production inefficiency but also breeds dissatisfaction with agriculture among

Table 43. Distribution of female family workers by major industrial sector: 1995

Major industrial sector	Number	Percentage
Agriculture, forestry and fisheries	1 242 484	35.9
Wholesale and retail trade etc.	1 017 791	29.4
Services	473 597	13.7
Manufacturing	362 228	10.5
Construction	224 767	6.5
Other sectors	136 295	3.9
Total	3 457 162	100.0

Source: Statistics Bureau, Management and Coordination Agency, *1995 Population Census of Japan* (Tokyo, Government of Japan, 1997).

women. Hence, the Government has organized seminars for female agricultural workers since 1977, implemented special projects to promote the education of farming women since 1979 and established an agricultural women's centre to promote research and disseminate information. In order to improve the management abilities of women engaged in agriculture, a manual on farm planning and management efficiency has been compiled. The average proportion of female students among the entrants to prefectural farmers' academies increased from 10 per cent during the period 1985-1989 to 12.4 per cent in 1990-1991 and to about 15 per cent in 1992-1993.

3. Wages and remuneration

Although the principle of non-discrimination in regard to remuneration between male and female employees is ingrained in article 4 of the Labour Standards Law, available evidence indicates that the wages and remuneration received by female workers are, on the average, considerably lower than those of male workers in Japan. A 1988 ILO study covering industrialized countries determined that the male-female wage gap was highest in Japan, where the earnings of women workers constituted on the average about 50 per cent of the earnings of male workers. While most industrialized countries have recorded a narrowing in the gender gap in wages, in Japan the gap actually widened between 1980 and 1988. The Basic Survey on Wage Structure conducted by the Statistics Bureau in 1990, however, revealed that the salary levels of women workers were about 60 per cent of those of male workers.

Enquiries conducted by the Ministry of Labour also confirm considerable differences in wages between males and females, even with similar educational attainment, in both large and small establishments. In 1990, for instance, the wages of female high-school graduates as a proportion of the corresponding wages of males averaged 67.5 per cent in large establishments and 64.1 per cent in smaller establishments. Similarly, the wages of female university graduates constituted 57.1 per cent of the corresponding wages of males in large firms and 74.1 per cent in small firms (table 44).

According to information collected by the Ministry of Labour, gender differentials in earnings also vary considerably from one industrial sector to another. In 1994, this differential was most pronounced in the trade sector, where the gross annual earnings of a female regular employee were only about 41 per cent of the earnings of her male counterpart, and the gap in earnings was narrowest in the mining, transport and communications and service sectors, where the earnings of female employees formed around 61 per cent of the earnings of male employees (table 45).

Gender differentials in wages also exist among full-time and part-time employees, this differential being more marked in the case of part-time compared with full-time employees. For instance, in 1990, the average wages paid to a female employee as a percentage of the wages of a male employee were 53.4 per cent in respect of part-time employment and 61.2 per cent in respect of full-time employment (table 46).

All available evidence clearly points to the fact that in Japan, women's wages/earnings are, on the average, considerably lower than those of men. This inequality has been attributed to differences in fields of employment, length of service and academic background between male and female workers. In Japan, as in most other countries, a substantially higher proportion of males compared with females are engaged in high-level occupations in the fields of science, technology, engineering and medicine, which require skills of a very high level and carry a very high level of remuneration. On the other hand, the majority of women employees are concentrated in occupations that require relatively low skills and hence involve relatively low pay.

Second, remuneration is influenced by seniority, which is a very important aspect of the Japanese wage system. Available data indicate that the average monthly contractual earnings for males increase gradually from the

Table 44. Female wages[a/] as a percentage of male wages by size of firm and by educational attainment of workers: 1975 to 1990

Year	Large firms			Small firms		
	High-school graduates	University graduates	Total	High-school graduates	University graduates	Total
1975	68.1	67.1	64.9	61.9	74.8	59.2
1980	62.1	55.8	58.7	63.7	75.6.	60.3
1985	63.9	59.7	60.8	63.9	75.5	61.7
1990	67.5	57.1	62.3	64.1	74.1	62.5

Source: Ministry of Labour, *Wage Census* (various years).

[a/] Including bonus payments.

50

Table 45. Average gross annual earnings of regular employees by industrial sector and sex[a/]: 1994

(Thousands of yen)

Industrial sector	Total earnings			Contractual earnings[b/]		
	Male	Female	Female as percentage of male	Male	Female	Female as percentage of male
Mining	5 441	3 302	60.7	4 101	2 363	57.6
Construction	5 823	2 944	50.6	4 416	2 258	51.1
Manufacturing	5 548	2 410	43.4	4 158	1 902	45.7
Electricity, gas and water	7 366	3 896	52.9	5 258	2 802	53.3
Transport and communications	5 713	3 510	61.4	4 377	2 628	60.0
Wholesale and retail trade, eating and drinking establishment	5 535	2 253	40.7	4 129	1 814	43.9
Finance and insurance	8 678	3 958	45.6	6 016	2 888	48.0
Real estate	6 782	2 921	43.1	4 895	2 244	45.8
Services	5 941	3 649	61.4	4 380	2 756	62.9
All industrial sectors	5 837	2 989	51.2	4 349	2 298	52.8

Source: Ministry of Labour.

[a/] Covering establishments with 30 or more regular employees.

[b/] Including family allowances, overtime payments, cost of living allowances, and others.

Table 46. Average wages of females as a percentage of wages of males in full-time and part-time employment: 1970 to 1990

Year	Female wages as a percentage of male wages	
	Full-time employees	Part-time employees
1970	55.4	57.4
1975	61.2	59.4
1980	59.1	52.6
1985	60.1	54.1
1990	61.2	53.4

Source: Ministry of Labour.

In the context of the seniority-based wage system that has traditionally characterized the Japanese employment market, the withdrawal of women from work when they marry or when they have children was considered to be a way of keeping the labour costs at low levels. But today, with women attaining educational levels higher than those of men, labour laws mandating maternity and child-raising leave, and with care for infants provided by public day-care centres, an increasing number of women delay their retreat from the labour force. It is, therefore, very likely that a substantial narrowing in gender wage differentials will occur in the near future.

youngest age group (15-17 years) up to ages 50-54 years, and that the wages of workers aged 50-54 years are almost twice as high as those of workers aged 20-24 years. However, in the case of females, the wages do not show such marked differences by age groups. This is largely due to the fact that since women withdraw from the labour force upon marriage or childbirth, and re-enter it when their children start going to school, they lose their seniority in employment, which is determined by continuous service.

4. Unemployed persons

In Japan, the "unemployed" refers to those who have no job but are able to work and actually seeking work during the time reference period of one week preceding the census/survey. The number of unemployed persons by sex as reported in the labour-force surveys from 1980 to 1995 is shown in annex table E.1. The unemployment rate (or the unemployed as a proportion of the labour force) by sex is given in table 47.

Table 47. Unemployment rate by sex: 1980 to 1995

Year	Unemployment rate (percentage)		
	Both sexes	Male	Female
1980	2.0	2.0	2.0
1985	2.6	2.6	2.7
1990	2.1	2.1	2.2
1995	3.1	3.1	3.2

Source: Statistics Bureau, Management and Coordination Agency, *Labour Force Survey* (various years).

It will be noted from table 47 that the overall unemployment rate rose from 2.0 per cent in 1980 to 3.1 per cent in 1995, and that during this 15-year period, the unemployment rate was almost the same for both males and females. The 1995 unemployment rate of 3 per cent is unprecedentedly high for Japan but still low by international standards.

The unemployment rate has been increasing with the worsening of the employment situation for both men and women owing to the recession in the Japanese economy. During the summer of 1994, there were widespread reports that firms were clearly favouring male job applicants amidst a prolonged recession. Young women complained that they could not even get an interview, much less a job offer, while recent male graduates were cultivated by personnel officers as assiduously as in the past. This would indicate that the voluntary compliance urged in the Equal Employment Opportunity Law is inadequate to address the substantial problems women face in achieving equality in the labour market. It is, therefore, feared that if the current recession were to continue, unemployment would become a more serious problem for women than for men.

In Japan, unemployment benefits are provided to unemployed workers, regardless of gender, under the Employment Insurance System, in order to secure their living conditions and promote their search for new work. Basic allowances and other unemployment benefits are provided to any insured person who qualifies, in principle, for a period of 90 to 300 days. The duration of the benefits may be extended in the case of trainees in public vocational training, and others with special individual circumstances.

F. WOMEN IN PUBLIC LIFE

1. Women in politics

(a) Women as voters

In Japan, women were granted the right to vote and to be elected to public office on 17 December 1945. Since then, an increasing number of women have been registering as voters and have become eligible to exercise their franchise at various national as well as local-level elections. Available data indicate that women have consistently outnumbered men as registered or eligible voters at the various elections to the House of Representatives and the House of Councillors held during the past three decades. Women constituted 51.5 per cent of the total eligible voters at the 1993 elections to the House of Representatives as well as at the 1995 elections to the House of Councillors (table 48).

Data from the Election Department clearly show that the percentage of eligible voters actually exercising their voting rights, or the voter turnout rate, was also slightly higher among women than men at each of the nine elections for the House of Representatives held between 1969 and 1993, as well as at each of the nine elections for the House of Councillors held between 1968 and 1992. In other words, more women than men have actually gone to the polls during the past more than two decades (table 49 and annex table F.1)

(b) Women in parliament

Although women constitute a slightly higher proportion among all registered or eligible voters as well as among all actual voters, they continue to be grossly under-represented in both chambers of the national parliament (Diet). As at January 1960, females accounted for 2.4 per cent of the 467 members of the House

Table 48. Eligible voters as of election day by sex: House of Representatives and House of Councillors

(Thousands)

| | House of Representatives | | | | | House of Councillors | | | |
| | Eligible voters (thousands) | | | | | Eligible voted (thousands) | | | |
Date of election	Both sexes	Male	Female	Percent-age female	Date of election	Both sexes	Male	Female	Percent-age female
11 November 1963	58 282	27 884	30 398	**52.2**	7 July 1965	59 544	28 500	31 044	**52.1**
1 January 1967	62 993	30 245	32 748	**52.0**	7 July 1968	65 886	31 710	34 177	**51.9**
12 December 1969	69 260	33 461	35 799	**51.7**	6 June 1971	71 178	34 412	36 766	**51.7**
12 December 1972	73 770	35 671	38 099	**51.6**	7 July 1974	75 356	36 451	38 905	**51.6**
12 December 1976	77 927	37 724	40 203	**51.6**	7 July 1977	78 322	37 911	40 410	**51.6**
10 October 1979	80 170	38 802	41 368	**51.6**	6 June 1980	80 925	39 171	41 754	**51.6**
6 June 1980	80 925	39 171	41 754	**51.6**	6 June 1983	83 682	40 520	43 162	**51.6**
12 December 1983	84 253	40 804	43 448	**51.6**	7 July 1986	86 427	41 842	44 585	**51.6**
7 July 1986	86 427	41 842	44 585	**51.6**	7 July 1989	89 891	43 557	46 334	**51.5**
2 February 1990	90 323	43 768	46 555	**51.5**	7 July 1992	93 254	45 225	48 029	**51.5**
7 July 1993	94 478	45 828	48 650	**51.5**	7 July 1995	96 759	46 957	49 802	**51.5**

Source: Election Department, Local Administration Bureau, Ministry of Home Affairs.

Table 49. Percentage of eligible voters actually voting at elections for the House of Representatives and the House of Councillors, by sex

| | House of Representatives | | | | House of Councillors | | |
| | Voter turnout rate (percentage) | | | | Voter turnout rate (percentage) | | |
Date of election	Both sexes	Male	Female	Date of election	Both sexes	Male	Female
11 November 1963	71.1	72.4	70.0	7 July 1965	67.0	68.0	66.1
1 January 1967	74.0	74.8	73.3	7 July 1968	68.9	68.9	69.0
12 December 1969	68.6	67.6	69.1	6 June 1971	59.2	59.1	59.3
12 December 1972	71.8	71.0	72.5	7 July 1974	73.2	72.7	73.6
12 December 1976	73.4	72.8	74.0	7 July 1977	68.5	67.7	69.3
10 October 1979	68.0	67.4	68.6	6 June 1980	74.5	73.7	75.3
6 June 1980	74.6	73.7	75.4	6 June 1983	57.0	56.9	57.1
12 December 1983	67.9	67.6	68.3	7 July 1986	71.3	70.1	72.4
7 July 1986	71.4	70.2	72.5	7 July 1989	65.0	64.4	65.3
2 February 1990	73.3	71.9	74.6	7 July 1992	50.7	50.6	50.8
7 July 1993	67.3	66.4	68.1	7 July 1995	44.5	44.7	44.4

Source: Election Department, Local Administration Bureau, Ministry of Home Affairs.

of Representatives, and 5.2 per cent of the 250 members of the House of Councillors, or 3.3 per cent of the total 717 Diet members. Thirty-four years later, in January 1994, women accounted for only 2.7 per cent of the total membership of the House of Representatives and 15.1 per cent of all members of the House of Councillors, or 6.8 per cent of all Diet members (table 50). Thus, there has been no worthwhile improvement in the participation of women in the highest-level legislative body of the country. Indeed, the percentage share of females in the total number of legislators in Japan is the lowest among the industrialized countries of the world.

Since only a few women are elected as members of parliament, women are also very much under-represented in positions of responsibility within the parliamentary system. Until very recently, no Japanese women had served as Speaker or Vice-Speaker in either of the

Table 50. Distribution of parliament (Diet) members by chamber and sex: 1960 to 1994

Year	House of Representatives				House of Councillors				Total (Diet)			
	Both sexes	Male	Female	Percent-age female	Both sexes	Male	Female	Percent-age female	Both sexes	Male	Female	Percent-age female
1960	467	456	11	2.4	250	237	13	5.2	717	693	24	3.3
1965	467	460	7	1.5	250	234	16	6.4	717	694	23	3.2
1970	486	478	8	1.6	250	237	13	5.2	736	715	21	2.9
1975	491	484	7	1.4	252	234	18	7.1	743	718	25	3.4
1980	511	500	11	2.2	250	234	16	6.4	761	734	27	3.5
1985	511	503	8	1.6	249	231	18	7.2	760	734	26	3.4
1990	512	505	7	1.4	252	219	33	13.1	764	724	40	5.2
1994	512	498	14	2.7	252	214	38	15.1	764	712	52	6.8

Source: Secretariats of the House of Representatives and the House of Councillors.

Houses of the Diet, and no woman has ever held the post of Prime Minister in the constitutional history of Japan. Even as recently as 1994, only 3 of the 21 ministerial positions and 2 of the 23 vice-ministerial positions were held by women.

In view of their relatively better representation in the House of Councillors, at least one woman is appointed to each Standing Committee, with a comparatively larger number of women serving on committees that deal with matters traditionally associated with women, such as education, health, welfare, labour and the environment. In the House of Representatives, women are seldom appointed to the standing committees relating to the Cabinet, local administration, finance, transport, construction, and the Steering Committee for Parliamentary Proceedings.

The very poor representation or participation of women in the political process could be attributed to several factors. Foremost among these is the persistence of rigid societal concepts of differential gender roles. Most Japanese, particularly men, are still of the view that voting is an appropriate action for women but running in an election and being active in political life is not. It is often argued that assertiveness and ability to present arguments and proof and to maintain dialogue and negotiate tenaciously, all of which are necessary to succeed in politics, are unwomanly and inappropriate behaviour for women.

Second, women are often discriminated against in the selection of candidates for election by party leaders, who are invariably men. This discrimination arises from the concept of sex-role differentiation referred to earlier and the traditional image of women held by the majority of Japanese men. A glaring example of this is often noted in the selection of candidates to run for election to the House of Councillors. Since 1983, Japan has adopted the proportional representation system based on a prioritized list of candidates prepared by each of the contesting political parties. Thus, candidates placed high on the prioritized list have a better chance of being elected than those named lower down an the list. It is well known that party leaders usually give priority to male candidates and that women candidates are placed in hopelessly lower positions on the list, thereby jeopardizing their chances of being elected.

Third, the personalization and privatization of electorates result in an increase in the number of hereditary male politicians. The political allegiance and behaviour of Japanese people are based mostly on personality rather than on considerations of policies and programmes. The political process of selecting candidates, and thus the outcome of elections, is a highly personalized process. Politicians tend to cultivate their electorates by granting personal favours such as finding jobs, arranging marriages, and presiding at funerals, in addition to constructing roads, bridges, railways etc. in their electorates. In this way, they ensure that upon their retirement from political life owing to old age or ill health, or upon their death, their male descendents can become their successors. However, in very rare instances, the wives of politicians who compaigned actively for their husbands have stood for election upon the death of their husbands and been elected on grounds of sympathy.

Fourth, the high cost of election campaigns also deters women from coming forward as candidates. Although officially the cost of standing for an election is not very high, in actual practice elective politics is a very expensive process which most of the capable women cannot afford.

Fifth, there is also a shortage of support networks for women politicians. Although there are many protest groups, interest groups and citizens' groups among women activists, most of these groups are very small, and do not form a united front to support women politicians. Further, while it is true that a higher proportion among women than men actually vote at elections, women voters do not necessarily support or vote for women candidates.

Sixth, the repeated occurrence of political corruption has resulted in rising apathy among women voters, particularly the younger generation, who have come to condemn politics as a dirty business.

Nevertheless, in recent years attempts have been made to increase the participation of women in the political process as well their relative share in the membership of elected bodies. Political parties have begun to recruit and support female candidates and have even introduced quotas with respect to the proportion of female candidates to serve in the party executive bodies and to be nominated as candidates to run in elections. On their part, women's groups at all levels have also been expanding their activities to make it possible for the voices of women to be heard in national and local-level politics. These activities include lobbying political parties, supporting female candidates, studying the election system and taking part in various campaigns.

(c) Women in local government

Available data indicate that the total number of women in all local assemblies more than trebled, from 681 in 1975 to 2,238 in 1993, and their relative share went from 0.9 to 3.4 per cent during the same period. However, this increase varied from one type of local assembly to another. Between 1975 and 1993, the proportionate share of women increased from 1.1 to 2.6 per cent in prefectural assemblies; from 1.8 to 5.9 per cent at the city level; from 0.5 to 2.2 per cent at the town and village level; and from 6.6 to 12.1 per cent in special ward assemblies (annex table F.2).

Although the participation of women in local government assemblies is quite low, their increase in the total membership of the various assemblies is quite significant. This increase has been made possible by efforts similar to those mentioned earlier with regard to participation in national-level politics. That is, political parties have made efforts to recruit and support female candidates, and women, both as individuals and as members of organizations, have striven to increase their participation in local assemblies in order to make their views known on issues related to their community and personal lives.

Since women are grossly under-represented in the local-level assemblies, they fail to be elected as heads of these assemblies. It will be noted from table 51 that in 1993, there were no women prefectural governors, and no women heads of special wards, while only two of the 662 city mayors and one of the 2,570 heads of towns and villages were women.

2. Women in government service

According to data from the National Personnel Authority, there was a slight increase in the number of women employed as regular public service employees, from 34,844 in 1980 to 36,032 in 1992. Nevertheless, women continue to be grossly under-represented in this employment sector, their relative share among total regular government employees having increased only minimally, from 14.0

Table 51. Number of prefectural governors, mayors of cities, and heads of special wards, towns and villages, by sex: 1980 and 1993

Position	1980			1993		
	Both sexes	Male	Female	Both sexes	Male	Female
Prefectural governor	47	47	–	47	47	–
Mayor of city	644	644	–	662	660	2
Head of special ward	22	22	–	23	23	–
Town and village head	2 608	2 606	2	2 570	2 569	1

Source: Ministry of Home Affairs.

per cent in 1980 to 15.4 per cent in 1992 (table 52).

The substantial under-representation of women in the civil service of Japan is largely due to the fact that for a long time only men were eligible to sit for the entrance examinations for recruitment to six job categories. It was only in 1989 that the Government removed the gender restriction and women became eligible to appear for the entrance examinations.

Available data also indicate that not only are women very much under-represented in government service, but a vast majority of them are also concentrated in the lowest rungs or levels of this service. In 1993, nearly 58 per cent of all female regular public service employees were in grades 1-3 of the service, the corresponding proportion among males being only about 35 per cent (table 53).

In 1992, significant changes were made by removing the restrictions against women taking the examinations for entrance into the National Defence Academy and the National Defence Medical College. The Academy also reviewed its policy on the assignment of female Self-defence Force personnel in order to expand their service areas and thus better utilize their potential. Consequently, the Academy has allowed women to take the entrance examination for recruitment for the Maritime Self-defence Forces, and the Air Self-defence Forces, beginning in 1993. As a result of these developments, the number of female Self-defence personnel more than doubled, from 3,690 in 1985 to 8,880 in 1993. Nevertheless, women constitute only about 4 per cent of all self-defence personnel in the country (table 54).

Although the number of female police officers increased substantially from 3,700 in 1980 to 5,500 in 1993, they are still very much under-represented in the national police force. In 1993, women constituted 2.5 per cent of the total police force, the corresponding proportion in 1980 being 1.8 per cent (table 55).

Table 52. Regular public service employees by sex: selected years, 1980 to 1992

Year	Number of employees			Percentage female
	Both sexes	Male	Female	
1980	248 494	213 650	34 844	14.0
1985	245 386	210 812	34 574	14.1
1990	233 834	198 926	34 908	14.9
1992	233 489	197 457	36 032	15.4

Source: National Personnel Authority, *Report on Survey of Recruitment in the National Regular Public Service.*

Table 53. Distribution of regular public service employees by grade and sex: 1980 and 1992

Grades	1980						1992					
	Both sexes		Male		Female		Both sexes		Male		Female	
	Number	Percentage	Number	Percentage	Number	Percentage	Number	Percentage	Number	Percentage	Number	Percentage
1-3	102 624	41.3	79 289	37.1	23 335	67.0	90 199	38.6	69 458	35.2	20 741	57.6
4-8	138 014	55.5	126 543	59.2	11 471	32.9	134 360	57.5	119 132	60.3	15 228	42.3
9-11	6 337	2.6	6 301	2.9	36	0.1	7 257	3.1	7 203	3.6	54	0.1
Designated service	1 519	0.6	1 517	0.7	2	–	1 673	0.7	1 664	0.8	9	–
Total	248 494	100.0	213 650	100.0	34 844	100.0	233 489	100.0	197 457	100.0	36 032	100.0

Source: National Personnel Authority, *Report on Survey of Recruitment in the National Regular Public Service.*

Table 54. Self-defence Force personnel by sex: 1980, 1985 and 1993

Year[a]	Number of (Self-defence Force) personnel[b]			Percentage female
	Both sexes	Male	Female	
1980	241 960	238 890	3 070	1.3
1985	245 420	241 730	3 690	1.5
1993	233 820	224 940	8 880	3.8

Source: Defence Academy.

[a] As of the end of each fiscal year.
[b] The number of personnel are rounded to the nearest 10 persons.

Table 55. Distribution of police officers by sex: 1980, 1985 and 1993

Year	Number of police officers[a]			Percentage female
	Both sexes	Male	Female[b]	
1980	210 638	206 938	3 700	1.8
1985	215 870	211 770	4 100	1.9
1990	221 085	215 585	5 500	2.5

Source: National Police Agency.

[a] Figures relating to police officers represent the authorized strength of police officers for prefectural police (including local senior police officers).

[b] The number of female police officers are approximate figures as at the beginning of each fiscal year.

The relative share of females in the total number of employees in the Ministry of Foreign Affairs increased from 12.7 per cent in 1985 to 14.8 per cent in 1994. The Ministry of Foreign Affairs has a tradition of hiring highly qualified female personnel, and the number of female diplomats recruited through the Foreign Service Personnel Examination and the Foreign Service Specialist Examination has increased steadily over the years. Nevertheless, only four women were designated as ambassadors in the Foreign Ministry in 1994.

3. Women in the judicial system

Between 1980 and 1994, the number of practising lawyers in Japan increased by about 27 per cent from 11,680 to 14,828, but this increase was more pronounced in the case of female compared with male lawyers. Whereas the number of practising male lawyers increased by 23.6 per cent, from 11,235 in 1980 to 13,889 in 1994, the number of female lawyers more than doubled, from 445 to 939, during the same period. Consequently, the relative share of females among the total practising lawyers increased from 3.8 per cent in 1980 to 6.3 per cent in 1994 (table 56).

Since only a few women take to the legal profession, women constitute a very small proportion of the public prosecutors and judges in the country. Although the number of female prosecutors more than doubled, from 25 in 1980 to 57 in 1993, women accounted for only about 3 per cent of the total cadre of public prosecutors in 1993. Further, of the 57 female public prosecutors in 1993, only 6, or 10.5 per cent, were in level I of this service, the corresponding proportion among males being 28 per cent (table 57).

Available data indicate that the combined total of female judges assistant judges increased dramatically, from 76 in 1980 to 204 in 1994, and this increase has resulted in a rise in their relative share in the total number of judges, from 2.8 to 7.2 per cent during the same 14-year period. However, in view of their relatively shorter length of service, the majority (60 per cent) of the females in the judiciary are serving as assistant judges (table 58).

4. Women in national advisory councils

Women's participation in decision-making processes is most essential to ensure that women's interests and concerns are fully taken into account in the formulation of official policies and programmes. In recognition of this fact, a minimum of 30 per cent representation of women at the decision-making level was set as a target to be achieved by 1995 in the Recommendations and Conclusions arising from

Table 56. Distribution of practising lawyers by gender: 1980, 1985 and 1994

Year	Number of practising lawyers[a]			Percentage female
	Both sexes	Male	Female	
1980	11 680	11 235	445	3.8
1985	12 870	12 252	618	4.8
1994	14 828	13 889	939	6.3

Source: Secretariat of the Japan Federation of Bar Associations.

[a] "Practising lawyers" refers to the registered members of the Japan Federation of Bar Associations.

Table 57. Distribution of public prosecutors by level and sex: 1980, 1985 and 1993

Year	Total			Level I			Level II		
	Both sexes	Female	Percent- age female	Both sexes	Female	Percent- age female	Both sexes	Female	Percent- age female
1980	2 129	25	1.2	537	5	0.9	1 592	20	1.3
1985	2 104	27	1.3	565	3	0.5	1 539	24	1.6
1993	2 048	57	2.8	566	6	1.1	1 482	51	3.4

Source: Ministry of Justice.

Table 58. Number of judges and assistant judges by sex: 1980, 1985 and 1994

Year	All judges			Judges			Assistant judges		
	Both sexes	Female	Percent-age female	Both sexes	Female	Percent-age female	Both sexes	Female	Percent-age female
1980	2 747	76	2.8	2 134	43	2.0	613	33	54
1985	2 792	93	3.3	2 183	49	2.2	609	44	7.2
1994	2 829	203	7.2	2 191	80	3.7	638	123	19.3

Source: Supreme Court.

the first review and appraisal of the implementation of the Nairobi Forward-looking Strategies for the Advancement of Women. Despite this accepted goal, female participation in the policy decision-making process in Japan continues to be at a low level by international standards.

The Special Activity Guidelines for the Promotion of Women's Participation in Policy Decision-making, established in 1977, set a target whereby the relative share of women in national advisory councils would be raised to 10 per cent over the next 10 years. However, available data indicate that women's share in the total membership of these councils reached only 4.1 per cent in 1980 and 5.5 per cent in 1985. The New National Plan of Action, revised in 1991, established a minimum target of 15 per cent for the proportion of women committee members. Despite the efforts made to achieve this target, the proportionate share of women in national advisory committees had increased to only 11.3 per cent as of 31 March 1994.

Members of the national advisory councils are generally divided into three categories: senior government officials, nominees of relevant organizations, and others, mainly experts and scholars in the relevant fields. As noted earlier, very few women occupy senior positions in the administrative hierarchy of the government, and women experts and scholars, particularly in natural sciences, are also very rare in Japan. Consequently, women are considerably under-represented in most national advisory councils.

In accordance with the decision made by the Headquarters for the Promotion of Gender Equality on 21 May 1996, attempts are being made to reach the goal of a minimum 20 per cent of female membership in national advisory councils before the end of financial year 2000. The National Plan of Action for the Promotion of a Gender-equal Society by the Year 2000 has also proposed several measures to promote the participation of women in national advisory councils and committees.

PART II
ANNEX TABLES

Table C.1 Percentage distribution of the population by five-year age group and sex: 1950, 1970 and 1995

Age group	1950		1970		1990		1995	
	Male	Female	Male	Female	Male	Female	Male	Female
0-4	13.9	12.8	8.9	8.1	5.5	5.1	5.1	4.7
5-9	12.0	11.2	8.2	7.6	6.4	5.8	5.5	5.0
10-14	10.9	10.2	7.9	7.3	7.3	6.7	6.3	5.8
15-19	10.6	10.0	9.0	8.5	8.4	7.7	7.2	6.6
20-24	9.4	9.2	10.4	10.1	7.4	6.9	8.3	7.6
25-29	6.8	7.9	8.8	8.6	6.7	6.4	7.3	6.8
30-34	5.8	6.7	8.2	7.9	6.5	6.2	6.6	6.3
35-39	5.8	6.3	8.1	7.8	7.6	7.2	6.4	6.1
40-44	5.4	5.4	7.2	6.9	8.8	8.4	7.4	7.1
45-49	5.0	4.7	5.2	6.0	7.4	7.2	8.6	8.2
50-54	4.2	3.9	4.2	5.0	6.6	6.5	7.2	7.0
55-59	3.4	3.2	4.0	4.5	6.2	6.3	6.3	6.3
60-64	2.7	2.8	3.4	3.7	5.3	5.6	5.8	6.0
65-69	1.9	2.3	2.7	3.0	3.6	4.6	4.8	5.3
70-74	1.3	1.8	1.9	2.2	2.6	3.6	3.1	4.3
75-79	0.7	0.9	1.0	1.4	2.0	2.9	2.1	3.2
80+	0.3	0.6	0.7	1.2	1.7	3.0	2.0	3.6
All ages	100.0	100.0	100.0	100.0	100.0	100.0	100.0	100.0

Source: United Nations, *The Sex and Age Distribution of the World Populations: The 1996 Revision* (New York, 1997).

Table C.2 Numerical distribution of the population aged 15 years and over by marital status and sex

(Thousands)

Marital status/sex	1960	1965	1970	1975	1980	1985	1990	1995
Male								
Single	10 963	12 221	12 358	11 946	12 383	13 652	15 271	16 264
Married	19 179	21 865	24 523	27 711	29 387	30 525	31 256	32 015
Widowed	1 109	1 054	1 015	1 053	1 061	1 124	1 175	1 308
Divorced	285	270	322	388	532	749	901	1 141
Total[a]	31 542	35 430	38 227	41 112	43 442	46 131	48 956	51 091
Female								
Single	9 099	10 205	10 112	9 376	9 617	10 486	12 150	13 053
Married	19 200	21 821	24 525	27 751	29 472	30 547	31 290	32 055
Widowed	4 784	4 927	5 188	5 518	5 717	6 182	6 396	7 056
Divorced	720	703	840	905	1 129	1 466	1 677	2 018
Total[a]	33 810	37 679	40 669	43 561	46 040	48 843	51 842	54 433

Source: Statistics Bureau, Management and Coordination Agency.

[a] Including marital status not reported.

Table C.3 Number of teachers by sex and level of education

A. School education: 1955-1995

Year	Elementary schools[a]			Lower secondary schools[a]			Upper secondary schools[a]		
	Both sexes	Male	Female	Both sexes	Male	Female	Both sexes	Male	Female
1955	340 572	182 333	158 239	199 062	153 417	45 645	111 617	91 932	19 685
1960	360 660	197 222	163 438	205 988	161 237	44 751	131 719	109 231	22 488
1965	345 118	178 218	166 900	237 750	177 534	60 216	193 524	160 158	33 366
1970	367 941	180 619	187 322	224 546	165 048	59 498	202 440	168 577	33 863
1975	415 071	187 813	227 258	234 844	165 801	69 043	222 915	184 950	37 965
1980	467 953	203 021	264 932	251 279	170 811	80 468	243 592	200 001	43 591
1985	461 256	203 037	258 219	285 123	188 409	96 714	266 809	216 824	49 985
1990	444 218	185 030	259 188	286 065	182 058	104 007	286 006	227 341	58 665
1995	430 958	167 332	263 626	271 020	164 683	106 337	281 117	215 792	65 325

B. Higher education: 1955-1995

Year	Junior colleges			Technical colleges			Universities		
	Both sexes	Male	Female	Both sexes	Male	Female	Both sexes	Male	Female
1955	12 200	9 879	2 321	..	..	..	51 769	49 359	2 410
1960	13 656	10 574	3 082	..	..	..	61 021	57 681	3 340
1965	20 451	15 207	5 244	..	..	..	83 204	77 613	5 591
1970	32 764	23 189	9 575	5 120	5 056	64	118 971	109 721	9 250
1975	35 924	24 995	10 929	5 778	5 688	90	147 285	135 115	12 170
1980	39 050	25 779	13 271	5 748	5 632	116	168 739	152 737	16 002
1985	44 953	29 609	15 344	5 909	5 763	146	189 016	170 211	18 805
1990	54 244	35 577	18 667	6 340	6 118	222	213 951	189 440	24 511
1995	58 947	37 362	21 585	6 808	6 472	336	250 132	216 205	33 927

Source: Ministry of Education, *School Basic Survey* (various years).

[a] Referring to full-time teachers only.

Table C.4 Percentage distribution of persons aged 25 years and over by educational attainment, sex and residence: 1990

Age group/residence		First level		Second level		Post-secondary		Total	
		Both sexes	Female	Both sexes	Female	Both sexes	Female	Both sexes	Female
25-34	Japan	7.2	5.7	50.0	52.8	42.8	41.5	100.0	100.0
	Urban	6.5	5.1	47.9	51.1	45.6	43.8	100.0	100.0
	Rural	10.2	8.3	48.6	60.0	31.2	31.7	100.0	100.0
35-44	Japan	19.6	19.0	53.5	58.3	27.0	22.7	100.0	100.0
	Urban	17.5	16.9	52.9	58.3	29.6	24.8	100.0	100.0
	Rural	27.1	26.6	55.3	58.4	17.6	15.0	100.0	100.0
45-54	Japan	36.5	38.4	48.1	51.2	15.4	10.4	100.0	100.0
	Urban	33.1	34.6	49.7	53.6	17.2	11.8	100.0	100.0
	Rural	49.2	52.3	42.4	42.3	8.4	5.4	100.0	100.0
55-64	Japan	47.9	47.1	40.9	47.2	11.3	5.7	100.0	100.0
	Urban	42.0	44.0	44.6	48.7	13.4	7.3	100.0	100.0
	Rural	64.6	54.0	30.3	43.7	5.1	2.3	100.0	100.0
65+	Japan	66.9	70.1	26.0	26.4	7.1	3.5	100.0	100.0
	Urban	61.9	65.7	29.4	30.1	8.7	4.2	100.0	100.0
	Rural	78.6	80.9	17.9	17.5	3.5	1.6	100.0	100.0
25+	Japan	34.3	36.0	44.5	47.3	21.2	16.7	100.0	100.0
	Urban	30.2	32.2	45.9	48.9	23.9	18.9	100.0	100.0
	Rural	47.5	47.8	40.0	42.5	12.5	8.7	100.0	100.0

Source: UNESCO, *Statistical Yearbook,* 1995.

Table C.5 Age-specific death rates by sex: selected years, 1970-1994

(Per thousand population)

Age (years)	1970		1980		1985		1990		1994	
	Male	Female	Male	Female	Male	Female	Male	Female	Male	Female
0	14.7	11.4	8.3	6.6	5.9	5.1	5.0	4.2	4.7	3.8
1	1.9	1.5	1.1	1.0	0.9	0.8	0.9	0.7	0.7	0.6
2	1.2	0.9	0.8	0.5	0.6	0.4	0.5	0.4	0.5	0.3
3	0.8	0.6	0.6	0.4	0.4	0.3	0.4	0.3	0.4	0.3
4	1.0	0.6	0.5	0.3	0.3	0.2	0.3	0.2	0.3	0.2
5-9	0.6	0.4	0.3	0.2	0.3	0.2	0.2	0.1	0.2	0.1
10-14	0.4	0.3	0.2	0.1	0.2	0.1	0.2	0.1	0.2	0.1
15-19	1.1	0.4	0.7	0.3	0.7	0.2	0.6	0.2	0.5	0.2
20-24	1.3	0.7	0.9	0.4	0.8	0.3	0.8	0.3	0.7	0.3
25-29	1.4	0.9	0.9	0.5	0.8	0.4	0.7	0.3	0.7	0.3
30-34	1.7	1.0	1.0	0.6	0.9	0.6	0.8	0.5	0.8	0.4
35-39	2.5	1.4	1.6	0.9	1.3	0.8	1.2	0.7	1.1	0.6
40-44	3.5	2.1	2.6	1.4	2.3	1.2	1.8	1.0	1.9	1.0
45-49	5.0	3.1	4.4	2.1	3.7	1.8	3.2	1.7	2.9	1.5
50-54	8.0	4.8	6.4	3.3	6.2	2.9	5.1	2.5	4.8	2.3
55-59	13.2	7.5	9.2	4.8	9.1	4.1	8.7	3.7	7.8	3.5
60-64	21.8	12.2	15.1	7.8	13.1	6.6	13.2	5.7	13.2	5.4
65-69	37.4	20.9	25.5	13.5	21.6	11.1	19.5	9.4	19.6	8.6
70-74	60.8	37.5	44.0	25.0	37.1	20.0	33.2	16.9	30.7	14.8
75-79	98.1	67.2	75.9	47.8	65.8	38.7	57.9	32.0	54.5	28.6
80-84	151.2	115.5	123.8	88.0	108.9	71.7	100.1	62.1	91.6	54.0
85-89	232.4	192.6	190.3	151.1	181.4	130.7	165.4	117.6	152.6	101.4
90+	297.7	285.5	296.8	263.2	254.3	224.9	268.0	216.1	251.6	191.9
All ages	7.7	6.2	6.8	5.6	6.9	5.6	7.4	6.0	7.8	6.3

Source: Ministry of Health and Welfare.

Table E.1 Population and labour force aged 15 years and over, by labour-force status and sex: 1980 to 1995

(Tens of thousands)

Year/sex	Population aged 15 years and over	Labour force aged 15 years and over			Persons aged 15 years and over not in labour force
		Total	Employed	Unemployed	
1980					
Both sexes	8 932	5 650	5 536	114	3 282
Male	4 341	3 465	3 394	71	876
Female	4 591	2 185	2 142	43	2 406
Percentage female	51.4	38.7	38.7	37.7	73.3
1985					
Both sexes	9 465	5 963	5 807	156	3 502
Male	4 602	3 596	3 503	93	1 006
Female	4 863	2 367	2 304	63	2 496
Percentage female	51.4	39.7	39.7	40.4	71.3
1990					
Both sexes	10 089	6 384	6 249	134	3 705
Male	4 911	3 791	3 713	77	1 120
Female	5 178	2 593	2 536	57	2 585
Percentage female	51.3	40.6	40.6	42.5	69.8
1995					
Both sexes	10 510	6 666	6 457	210	3 844
Male	5 108	3 966	3 843	123	1 142
Female	5 402	2 701	2 614	87	2 701
Percentage female	51.4	40.5	40.5	41.4	70.3

Source: Statistics Bureau, Management and Coordination Agency, *Labour Force Survey* (various years).

Table E.2 Labour-force participation rate by age and sex: 1965 to 1995

Age group	1965		1970		1975		1980		1985		1990		1995	
	Male	Fe-male	Male	Fe-male	Male	Fe-male	Male	Fe-male	Male	Fe-male	Male	Fe-male	Male	Fe-male
15-19	36.3	35.8	31.4	33.6	20.5	21.7	17.4	18.5	17.3	16.6	18.3	17.8	18.8	15.6
20-24	85.8	70.2	70.7	70.6	76.5	66.2	69.6	70.0	70.1	71.9	71.7	75.1	75.8	74.2
25-29	96.8	49.0	97.1	45.5	97.2	42.6	96.3	49.2	95.7	54.1	96.1	61.4	95.9	66.3
30-34	97.0	51.1	97.8	48.2	98.1	43.9	97.6	48.2	97.2	50.6	97.5	51.7	97.5	53.3
35-39	97.1	59.6	97.8	57.5	98.1	54.0	97.6	58.0	97.6	60.0	97.8	62.6	97.9	59.3
40-44	97.0	63.2	97.5	62.8	97.6	59.9	97.6	64.1	97.2	67.9	97.6	69.6	97.8	67.5
45-49	96.8	60.9	97.0	63.0	96.7	61.5	96.5	64.4	96.8	68.1	97.3	71.7	97.5	69.2
50-54	95.0	55.8	95.8	58.8	96.2	57.8	96.0	59.3	95.4	61.0	96.3	65.5	97.0	65.1
55-59	90.0	49.8	91.2	48.7	92.2	48.8	91.2	50.5	90.3	51.0	92.1	53.9	94.8	55.8
60-64	82.8	39.8	81.5	39.1	79.4	38.0	77.8	38.8	72.5	38.5	72.1	39.5	74.7	38.8
65+	56.3	21.6	49.4	17.9	44.4	15.3	41.0	15.5	37.0	15.5	36.5	16.2	41.9	15.7
Total	81.7	50.6	81.8	49.9	81.4	45.7	79.8	47.6	78.1	48.7	77.2	50.1	78.8	49.1

Source: Statistics Bureau, Management and Coordination Agency, *Labour Force Survey* (for the years 1965 to 1990) and *1995 Population Census of Japan.*

Table F.1 Number of eligible voters actually voting at various elections to the House of Representatives and House of Councillors, by sex

| | House of Representatives | | | | House of Councillors | | | |
| | Number actually voted (thousands) | | | | Number actually voted (thousands) | | |
Date of election	Both sexes	Male	Female	Date of election	Both sexes	Male	Female
11 November 1963	41 463	20 178	21 285	7 July 1965	39 901	19 371	20 530
1 January 1967	46 606	22 609	23 997	7 July 1968	45 418	21 845	23 573
12 December 1969	47 450	22 704	24 746	6 June 1971	42 161	20 349	21 810
12 December 1972	52 935	25 330	27 606	7 July 1974	55 158	26 512	28 646
12 December 1976	57 237	27 468	29 769	7 July 1977	53 635	25 648	27 987
10 October 1979	54 522	26 159	28 363	6 June 1980	60 299	28 858	31 441
6 June 1980	60 342	28 878	31 465	6 June 1983	47 696	23 050	24 646
12 December 1983	57 241	27 567	29 674	7 July 1986	61 643	29 347	32 296
7 July 1986	61 708	29 377	32 331	7 July 1989	58 434	28 029	30 405
2 February 1990	66 216	31 482	34 734	7 July 1992	47 284	22 864	24 419
7 July 1993	63 548	30 424	33 124	7 July 1995	43 060	20 969	22 091

Source: Election Department, Local Administration Bureau, Ministry of Home Affairs.

Table F.2 Membership of local assemblies by type of assembly and gender: 1975 to 1993[a]

| Type of local assembly | Year | Number of members | | | |
		Both sexes	Male	Female	Percentage female
Prefectural assembly	1975	2 828	2 796	32	1.1
	1980	2 833	2 799	34	1.2
	1985	2 857	2 819	38	1.3
	1993	2 839	2 766	73	2.6
City assembly	1975	20 167	19 807	360	1.8
	1980	20 080	19 639	441	2.2
	1985	19 729	19 128	601	3.0
	1993	19 130	17 996	1 134	5.9
Town and village assembly	1975	48 220	48 003	217	0.5
	1980	47 221	46 947	274	0.6
	1985	45 293	44 903	390	0.9
	1993	41 944	41 034	910	2.2
Special ward assembly	1975	1 088	1 016	72	6.6
	1980	1 073	1 000	73	6.8
	1985	1 032	959	73	7.1
	1993	1 004	883	121	12.1
All local assemblies	1975	72 303	71 622	681	0.9
	1980	71 207	70 385	822	1.2
	1985	68 911	67 809	1 102	1.6
	1993	64 917	62 679	2 238	3.4

Source: Ministry of Home Affairs.

[a] As of 31 December for each year.

REFERENCES

Economist Intelligence Unit (1995). *Japan: Country Profile, 1995-96* (London).

Economic and Social Commission for Asia and the Pacific (1984). *Population of Japan,* Country Monograph Series No. 11 (ST/ESCAP/269) (New York).

_____ (1987). *Achievements of the United Nations Decade for Women in Asia and the Pacific* (ST/ESCAP/434).

_____ (1995). *Population Change, Development and Women's Role and Status in Japan,* Asian Population Studies Series No. 133 (New York, United Nations).

Government of Japan (1992). *Country Statement of Japan: The Fourth Asian and Pacific Population Conference, 19-27 August 1992, Bali, Indonesia.*

_____ (1994). *National Report of the Government of Japan for the Fourth World Conference on Women.*

Hashimoto, Akiko (1997). "Designing family values: cultural assumptions of an aging society", *Japan Quarterly,* October-December.

Headquarters for the Promotion of Gender Equality (1996). *The National Plan of Action for Promotion of a Gender-equal Society by the Year 2000* (Tokyo, Office of the Prime Minister).

Jassey, Ikoko Anjo (1998). "Gender in elementary school texts", *Japan Quarterly,* January-March.

Kuroda, Toshio (1987). "Population aging in Japan with reference to China", *Asia-Pacific Population Journal,* vol. 2, No. 3.

Nagayama, Toshikazu (1995). "Japanese women: the participation of women in labour and the impact on Japanese society", in the Asian Population Development Association, *Women's Labour Participation and Economic Development in Asia: Strategy Toward 21st Century* (Tokyo).

Ogawa, Naohiro and Robert D. Retherford (1993). "Care of the elderly in Japan: changing norms and expectations", *Journal of Marriage and the Family,* vol. 55, No. 3.

Selvaratnam, S. (1988). "Population and status of women", *Asia-Pacific Population Journal,* vol. 3, No. 2.

Statistics Bureau, Management and Coordination Agency (1996). *Statistical Handbook of Japan, 1996* (Tokyo, Government of Japan).

_____ (1996). *Japan Statistical Yearbook, 1996* (Tokyo, Government of Japan).

_____ (1997a). *1995 Population Census of Japan,* vol. 3-1, *Labour Force Status of the Population, Industry (Major Groups) of Employed Persons* (Tokyo, Government of Japan).

_____ (1997b). *1995 Population Census of Japan,* vol. 4-1, *Occupation (Major Groups) of Employed Persons, Types of Households* (Tokyo, Government of Japan).

United Nations (1996). *Levels and Trends of Contraceptive Use as Assessed in 1994* (New York).

_____ (1997). *The Sex and Age Distribution of the World Populations: The 1996 Revision* (New York).

_____ (1998). *World Population Prospects: The 1996 Revision* (Sales No. E.98.XIII.5).